T&T CLARK STUDY GUIDES TO T

MARK

Series Editor
Tat-siong Benny Liew, College of the Holy Cross, USA

Other titles in the series include:

T&T Clark Study Guides to the Old Testament:

MARK

An Introduction and Study Guide
Shaping the Life and Legacy of Jesus

By
Abraham Smith

Bloomsbury T&T Clark
An imprint of Bloomsbury Publishing Plc

B L O O M S B U R Y
LONDON · OXFORD · NEW YORK · NEW DELHI · SYDNEY

Bloomsbury T&T Clark

An imprint of Bloomsbury Publishing Plc

Imprint previously known as T&T Clark

50 Bedford Square	1385 Broadway
London	New York
WC1B 3DP	NY 10018
UK	USA

www.bloomsbury.com

BLOOMSBURY, T&T CLARK and the Diana logo are trademarks of Bloomsbury Publishing Plc

First published 2015. This edition published 2017

© Abraham Smith, 2017

British Library Cataloguing-in-Publication Data
A catalogue record for this book is available from the British Library.

ISBN: PB: 978-1-3500-0887-8
ePDF: 978-1-3500-0889-2
ePub: 978-1-3500-0888-5

Library of Congress Cataloging-in-Publication Data
A catalog record for this book is available from the Library of Congress.

Series: T&T Clark Study Guides to the New Testament, volume 2

Cover design: clareturner.co.uk

Typeset by Newgen Knowledge Works (P) Ltd., Chennai, India
Printed and bound in Great Britain

For the unnamed and unheralded parade of
resilient resisters of civil wrongs in every age

CONTENTS

PREFACE

Ignored or rendered inferior for centuries, the Gospel of Mark did not receive much scrutiny until the rise of biblical criticism in the nineteenth century. Even then, though, the Gospel was embroiled in historical debates about the words and deeds of the historical Jesus, the content of early pre-Markan Christian proclamation, and the struggles of a local and specific Markan 'community'. For those interested in the historical Jesus, the Gospel of Mark was initially deemed as a reliable source to capture a pristine portrait of the Galilean. If, according to the Markan Priority Hypothesis of the period, Mark was written first and Matthew and Luke used Mark, scholars would turn to Mark to obtain the earliest written canonical Gospel witness about Jesus. This source-critical press for the earliest and most pristine Jesus, though, would be short-lived as the turn of the twentieth century soon revealed that Mark as an historical Jesus source—like Matthew and Luke—had theological biases that understandably serviced faith more than the annalistic record.

For those interested in pre-compositional Christian proclamation, the Gospel of Mark was said to be a window through which to observe the historical transmission and circulation of the oral traditions (or pre-literary formal units) that pre-dated Mark's actual composition. Yet, this enterprise bequeathed the composer of Mark the legacy of a scissors-and-paste person who haphazardly passed on the oral traditions without an overall sense for coherence or creativity. The whole enterprise (known as form criticism), moreover, presupposed discrete and successive moments in the oral transmission process that could not be verified with any extant texts. Thus, the so-called form critical 'rules' for the transmission process were imaginative but wholly unverifiable reconstructions.

For those interested in a so-called Markan community, as if the Gospel were addressed to a specific, localized community, the composer behind the work was a real author but the Gospel's primary value was the aid it could provide in reconstructing the historical concerns of that community. If scholars could separate the Markan redactor's editorial hand from what was assumed to be earlier source material, they could then posit the redactor's theological interests. Those interested in such theology (known as redaction critics) thus tried to read a distinctive feature of Mark's Gospel as if that feature indicated a concern in the Markan community. So, if Mark had a negative view of the disciples—compared to the other Synoptic Gospels (namely, Matthew and Luke, those Gospels that with Mark appear to view the basic story of Jesus similarly)—perhaps such a negative view reflected an actual errant ideology in the Markan community. This redaction critical approach, too, would soon be questioned because it assumed the Gospel was composed—like Paul's letters—for a fairly specific, localized community. This approach to the Gospel also assumed a correspondence between the negative portrait of the disciples and a hypothetical group in the Markan community apart from any substantive explorations on the literary function of negative depictions in Mark's literary environs.

Thus, not until the 1970s would the Gospel be appreciated for its own literary value, that is, as a creative and complete narrative. With the literary turn of the 1970s, scholars explored the Gospel's plot, characterization, narrative settings, and rhetorical persuasiveness. Some, building on a methodology based largely on modern-day novels, even went further as they teased the Gospel apart to separate the real flesh-and-blood author from the narrator on the one hand and from the implied author on the other. Such (narratology) scholars would view the Markan narrator simply as the teller of the story, the one able to furnish evaluative standards (often through privileged information, as in a prologue or through asides), and the one whose own perspective or point of view was not limited by time (with the narrator being able to hold together the past, present and future), space (with the narrator being able to be present in more than one place at the same time), or knowledge (with the narrator having extensive knowledge). Indeed, such scholars cast the Markan narrator as omniscient or as one who knew all the knowledge presupposed by a story's characters and much of the narrative's backstory and after-story. These scholars also understood the implied author to be the author that readers or auditors would be textually constrained to imagine on the basis of the information given in the text.

Whether or not twenty-first century scholars, including those interested in the Gospel's imperial social setting, were thoroughly wedded to the fairly technical developments of narratology in their analysis of Mark, most seemed genuinely influenced by the basic foundations laid earlier by literary critical investigations of the Gospel as a narrative whole. Thus, today the Gospel of Mark is no longer viewed as inferior. Its composer is no longer deemed as a scissors-and-paste person. The Gospel of Mark is now often recognized to be a rhetorically crafted work of art.

In accordance with the latest trends in Markan scholarship, this Guide also examines the Gospel as a narrative whole in its Roman imperial environment. The Guide presupposes that the Gospel of Mark is a complete and creative work. In making this kind of argument, the Guide seeks to take a different stance in its view of Mark's characterization of Jesus and of the disciples than what may be typical in some previous Markan studies.

This Guide assumes that Mark (by which I always mean the text and not the author [for whom there is not yet a convincing thesis]) largely is interested neither in the historical Jesus nor the historical disciples (and certainly not a pre-Markan transmission period). Accordingly, what readers of this textbook will find here then is a study dedicated to Mark's presentation of Jesus or, more precisely, to Mark's typological characterization of Jesus. Furthermore, the Guide offers no historical theses about the correction of an errant eschatology or an errant Christology, as if the portrait of the disciples pointed to the struggles of a sole localized 'community' addressed by the Gospel. Rather, Mark is a document that largely presents several characters as stylized, typological figures in order to help its auditors navigate their way through difficult times wherever they were.

My readers should note as well that the work presented here is not a comprehensive, encyclopedic characterization study. It offers only a provisional thesis on Mark's characterization of Jesus. In time, the thesis may be rejected, enhanced, or set in creative tension with other compelling theses. Yet, my work does seek to explore some of the socio-literary portraits through which Mark enhanced its depiction of Jesus. Though some attention is given to characterization theory in the introduction, the study largely sacrifices a steady diet of theory on the various methodological prisms for reading Mark to make Mark more manageable and palatable for wider public consumption. It also avoids the tedium of speculation about the specific historical circumstances behind the Gospel of Mark and settles for what I hope many Markan interpreters would see as a broad base of agreement: that the Gospel of Mark was written in first century CE imperial times (c. 66–70 CE) and that its author seeks to respond in some way to the power complexes of the Roman empire. I also presuppose that 'history' is always a rhetorical reconstruction that selects some items from the past as salient and worthy of consideration while much more lies dormant, distant, and often unvoiced until different focal prisms, reading strategies, and interpretive communities give visibility and voice to these remains.

Unless otherwise noted, the translations of Mark are my own. Also, unless otherwise noted, the translations outside of New Testament (most of which are based on the Loeb Classical Library) are also my own. Occasionally, transliterations of Greek texts are offered, especially when doing so will clarify intra-textual and inter-textual connections that would otherwise go unnoticed.

Reading Mark has been both a constant source of joy and a perennial labor of love. A labor of love such as this textbook, though, could not have been accomplished by a single author or mind. So, while the stylistic limitations of the Guide's series certainly make it impossible to acknowledge all the scholarship that informs my work, a debt of gratitude is owed to many Markan interpreters. Attentive readers will observe that the fount from which flows most of my understanding of Mark is the work of Mary Ann Tolbert whose scholarship on Mark has led a generation or more of scholars from Vanderbilt University to Pacific School of Religion to read the Gospel with literary and historical perspectives held in tandem. One of those scholars so nurtured by Tolbert is Tat-siong Benny Liew without whose editorial invitation and later vision this work would not have seen the light of day. Countless students have also shaped my thinking about Mark. One Hebrew Bible PhD student, Julián Andrés González Holguín, assisted me by reviewing an early form of the manuscript and creating the volume's indexes. From all these supporters, I have learned much. One M.Div. student, Kristopher Keller, proofed the galleys with a meticulous attention to detail. A budding scholar in his own right, Kris also offered invaluable editorial assistance to make the Guide a more reader-friendly document. Whatever mistakes remain in the Guide are, however, solely of my own making.

A hearty thanks is also owed to the Perkins School of Theology of Southern Methodist University for a 2012 sabbatical leave that afforded me the time for research and for the compilation of many Bible studies. The Bridwell Library staff at Southern Methodist University should be thanked as well for their assistance in securing additional resources in the Greek and Latin classics. Many laity groups and churches in the United States, one church in Santiago, Chile, and several seminaries in Brazil also helped me to hone my ideas about Mark. *Muchas gracias*! *Muito obrigado*!

My life would be incomplete without the heart and hope of those I call family. My siblings (Jeffrie, George, Mattie, Charles, and their families) are the 'wind beneath my wings'. They are all better people than I could ever hope to be. Two women who did not birth me took up the role my mother (Pauline Robinson Smith) could not complete because of death so early in life. One, Ida Mae Chapman, taught me to believe that God cared. Another, Georgiana Williams of blessed memory, taught me to believe that God was wise. Both, in their own ways, have been messengers of good news. I have always been blessed with the best of friends: Mario Rodriguez, Umesh Bhuju, Betty Ragan, the Reverend Zina Jacque, Evelyn Brooks Higginbotham, the late Reverend Reginald Billups, Peter Nguyen, and Bishop Sylvester Williams of the CME Church. I am a better person because each of you taught me to face the tyrannical pressures of life with courage.

Courage under pressure could well have been the theme of Mark's Gospel. So, let the creative and complete story be told! Let us explore Mark's story, 'the beginning of the good news' (Mk 1.1).

ABBREVIATIONS

BibInt	*Biblical Interpretation: A Journal of Contemporary Approaches*
CBQ	*Catholic Biblical Quarterly*
HTR	*Harvard Theological Review*
JBL	*Journal of Biblical Literature*
SBL Seminar Papers	Society of Biblical Literature Seminar Papers
SNTSMS	Society for New Testament Studies Monograph Series
TAPA	*Transactions of the American Philological Association*

The Markan narrative, 'the beginning of the good news' (1.1), is a story about Jesus as a teacher. As much as the story is *about* Jesus, though, it is also a story *for* others, that is, for Jesus' followers. It appears to have been written to assist others who may have been hustled up before the authorities on trumped up charges (13.9-13). How would the teacher's followers face such moments? Given the way Jesus died (an ignominious death on a cross), how could his followers know that his movement was not ultimately the failed ventures of a teacher and his immediate successors? Living in the shadows or threat of such infamy themselves, how could the Markan Jesus model for Mark's earliest auditors the way to endure tyrannical forces in the face of pressures in their own times?

This textbook presupposes that the Gospel's earliest auditors needed reasons to stay within the movement, to endure to the end despite the possible prevailing negative and shameful perceptions about Jesus and his movement (13.13; cf. 8.38). So, the Gospel *about* Jesus the teacher is also the Gospel that provided an inspirational paradigm *for* Mark's earliest auditors. In providing that inspiration, Mark's narrative both acknowledges the humiliation and seeming failure of Jesus' movement even as it rehabilitates perceptions about a crucified Jesus and his movement. Mark's Gospel then acknowledges what appeared to be signs of failure: fickle and frightened disciples (4.35-41; 14.50-52), a fractured fellowship (14.26-31, 66-72), and a near nauseating sequence of rituals of humiliation all dealt by Pilate and his henchmen (from the purple cloak, the mocking crown, and the empty salute to the scepter with which Jesus was struck, 15.15-20). Woven throughout the Markan narrative, though, are ancient public relations efforts—some too few and too weak for the later writers of the Gospels of Luke or Matthew—to elevate the status of Jesus and the potential status of his movement. In effect, Mark reshapes the memory of Jesus and his movement.

This textbook thus will argue that the Markan narrative rehabilitates the image of the crucified Jesus in the light of three interrelated characterization typologies (Jesus as a Prophetic Envoy, Jesus as a Powerful Broker, and Jesus as a Philosophical Hero). These typologies (or 'pre-existing character types in mythology, history, or literature' [De Temmerman 2007: 85]) assisted Mark's earliest auditors in hearing both a Markan story *about Jesus* and a Markan story for *Jesus' followers*, a story for their inspiration. So, on the one hand, the aforementioned characterization typologies likely rehabilitated the image of a crucified Jesus to distinguish him from other philosophers or powerful figures in a competitive social setting in which some influential leaders could still have been perceived as failures. On the other hand, such typologies likely also created a rich texture of exemplary values that Mark's earliest audiences would have embraced to prepare themselves to endure scrutiny and ignominy in whatever times they lived and in whatever places they lived. In some ways, the Markan narrative is also a story *against* something. As the three typologies are explored, the horizons of what the Gospel is against will become clearer, namely, the use of abusive power.

To argue this thesis, a few general remarks must be stated about characterization in the ancient world. *First*, today's readers need to know that for the Markan author, the characterization craft did not work the way it sometimes does with modern novels. So, initially, this introduction offers brief remarks on the distinctive and historically specific features of the ancient characterization craft. *Second*, today's readers need to know more about the highly competitive social setting in which Mark's presentation of Jesus as a teacher was produced. Mark's characterization of Jesus as a teacher would not have automatically rendered Jesus as a paragon of virtue. Rather, Mark was composed in a competitive social setting, a context in which various teachers and their followers traded barbs with rival groups on how best to achieve virtue. Such barbs also embraced typological characterization, not necessarily historical depiction, with the Gospel of Mark likely both responding to possible polemical critiques of a crucified leader and rendering some scathing expressions of its own. These remarks about characterization stated, then, the introduction will briefly sketch the content of each of the textbook's five chapters and the conclusion that follows.

The Markan Narrative and Ancient Typological Characterization

All ancient narratives deployed typological characterization, a point visibly evident in the notable degree to which many extant biographies from the period featured a series of a single type of life, whether the life of an emperor (Suetonius, *Lives of the Twelve Caesars*), the life of a famous philosopher or teacher (Diogenes Laertius, *Lives of Eminent Philosophers*), the life of a statesman (e.g. Cornelius Nepos's *Lives of Eminent Commanders*, the precursor to Plutarch's *Parallel Lives*), and so forth. Similarly, the ancient novels reveled in types, 'and [did] not exploit the interiorities of character as a means of enhancing the believability [of the character]' (Morgan 1993: 228). As Morgan notes: 'Kings must act like kings, slaves like slaves' (1993: 228).

Thus, a character in a story is not an historical depiction in a post-Enlightenment sense. Ancient characterization did not seek to offer indisputable factual information about an otherwise historical figure. Rather, for ancient writers, a character is a compositional element that 'can be established [by interpreters] through reference to literary models' (Seo 2013: 4). So, just as narrative setting is a part of the plot or overall story line of a narrative, so is characterization. For ancient writers, then, characterization is 'a poetic device' (Seo 2013: 2). Ancient writers depicted characters on the basis of repertoires they would have shared with their audiences. At the least, then, characters in one narrative world intertextually allude back to characters in other earlier narrative worlds.

Allusions to characters or character groups in previous narrative worlds could also include allusions to the constellation of associates by whom a given protagonist from a previous narrative world was characterized. Mark's characterization of Herod Antipas the tetrarch (ruler of a fourth of a kingdom; cf. Josephus, *Jewish Antiquities* 17.188) as a 'king' (6.14, 22, 25-27), for example, makes sense if the Gospel's earliest auditors are being nudged to see the power dynamics associated with Herod Antipas, Herodias, and John as similar to the one respectively associated with King Ahab, Jezebel, and the prophet Elijah.

Of course, today's scholars may have their own compelling reasons for continuing to make a quest for the historical Jesus or one for the historical Herod Antipas or one for the historical disciples. In all honesty, though, the ancient productions of literary characters as narrative components consistently provided ancient audiences with models for emotional connections, emulation, inspiration or, at times, avoidance through allusions to previously known narrative worlds (Seo 2013: 1). A literary character was not produced in a story to offer a pristine perspective on the historical figure represented.

Accordingly, this study will not examine Mark's characterization as if Mark were presenting autonomous personalities, in sync with the popular study of so-called 'flat' and 'round' characters by E.M. Forster (1927), the oft-cited study of Shakespearean characters by A.C. Bradley (1949), and the study of the range and depth of characters by W.J. Harvey (1965), all of which treat literary characters as autonomous human beings and all of which are firmly rooted in humanistic thinking, moral psychology, and Western notions of a 'Cartesian' self (Seo 2013: 8). Rather, this study will examine various socio-literary models by which Mark may have shaped the character known as Jesus.

Mark's Social Setting and the Typological Characterization of Rival Movements

Composed near the beginning of the last third of the first century CE and on the chronological cusp of the shift from the Julio-Claudian emperors (whose rule ended with Nero but was immediately followed by the brief imperial rules of Galba, Otho and Vitellius) to the Flavian emperors (whose rule commenced with Vespasian), the Gospel of Mark was written at a time when various subsets of Judaism—presumably including Mark's earliest auditors—would have viewed themselves as philosophical types. Such a typology, for example, is visible elsewhere in Jewish traditions whether one thinks of the philosophical overtones of *4 Maccabees* (esp. 1.1; 5.7, 22-24), Philo's presentation of Moses as a Hellenistic philosopher (in *Life of Moses,* 1.45.13), his view that the Jews use the Sabbath to study philosophy (*Special Laws*, 2.61), his discussion of the Jewish philosophical group known as the Therapeutae (Philo, *Contemplative Life* 1.2), or Josephus's mention of such groups as the Essenes, the Sadducees, and the Pharisees as philosophical schools (Josephus, *Jewish War* 2.119-66; *Jewish Antiquities* 13.171-173, 289; 18.12-22; *Life* 10-11; cf. Mason and Helfield 2008: 217-18). As John J. Collins has noted, in the characterization of the major Jewish apocalyptic figures, Enoch, Daniel, Ezra and Baruch, there is a 'certain blurring of the distinction between sage and prophet' (Collins 1990: 343).

Christianity as a Philosophy and the Markan Jesus as a Teacher
Christianity as one of the subsets of Judaism no less regarded itself as a philosophy. Studies of the Gospel of Luke, for example, have shown that the Lukan author depicts Jesus as a type of Socrates (Sterling 2001: 395-400; Spencer 2008: 50), especially in Luke's 'passion' account. Similarly, the Lukan author's characterization of the early witnesses—Stephen and Paul—with Socratic ideals also supports the view that the early Christians thought of their movement as a philosophy (Alexander 1993: 31-64). Studies of Paul indicate Paul's use of psychagogic traditions associated with philosophers (Malherbe 1989: 68). According to Christopher Bryan, '[I]t is clearly the sage with whom he [the Markan Jesus] has most in common… More than one critic has noted similarities of form and content between the brief units in which much of the teaching of Jesus is presented, and the chreiae [i.e. brief anecdotes attributed to a character] that typically enshrined traditions about Diogenes the Cynic and other teachers' (1993: 37).

Mark certainly labels Jesus as a teacher. While the Gospel of Mark includes only a few lengthy collections of Jesus' teachings compared to the other Synoptic Gospels, 'teacher' is still one of Mark's favorite expressions for Jesus. The attribute 'teacher' (*didaskalos*) occurs twelve times in Mark's Gospel with the similar expression 'rabbi' (or *rabboni*) occurring three times (9.5; 10.51; 11.21). Jesus' own followers exploit the teacher/rabbi/*rabboni* attributes six times (4.38; 9.5; 9.38; 10.35; 11.21; 13.1); and the established authorities do so three times (12.14, 19, 32). These teacher attributes are used five times (5.35; 9.17; 10.17, 20; 10.51) by seekers (e.g. one of the persons who came with the news of the death of Jairus's daughter;

the man whose son had epilepsy; and the man who asked Jesus about eternal life). Jesus calls himself 'teacher' in 14.14. If Jesus is a teacher, moreover, his followers of various sorts (whether the twelve or others) are most often called 'disciples' (*mathētai*) or literally 'learners' (2.15-16, 23; 3.7, 9; 4.34; 5.31; 6.1, 29, 35, 41, 45; 7.2, 5, 17; 8.1, 4, 6, 10, 27, 33-34; 9.14, 18, 28, 31; 10.10, 13, 23-24, 46; 11.1, 14; 12.43; 13.1; 14.4, 12-14, 16, 32; 16.7). As a teacher, Jesus calls these disciples and prepares them for the struggles against demonic opposition, that is, against the pockets of resistance to the nearness of the reign of God (1.14-15; 3.13-19; 6.6b-13, 30).

While Mark features 'teaching' diction throughout the Gospel, at least two sections abound with 'teaching' notices. Accordingly, in Jesus' first miracle in 1.21-28, for example, the diction about Jesus' teaching is mentioned with almost nauseating redundancy: 'after entering into the synagogue, he was teaching. And they were astonished at his teaching, for he taught them as one having authority, and not as the scribes… "What is this? A new teaching?—with authority"' (1.21b-22, 27b). Similarly, in portraying the arrival of Jesus and the Galilean crowds into Jerusalem and the temple, Mark continues to depict Jesus as a teacher (11.17, 18; cf. 'rabbi', 11.21). In the whole of 12.13-37, Mark's auditors are treated to a flurry of diction about Jesus' role as a 'teacher' (12.14, 19, 32; 13.1) or about his 'teaching' (12.35, 38). Thus, the repetition of teaching diction provides thematic unity for all of 12.13–13.37 in association with the first mention of his teaching in the temple (11.17). Indeed, later, with a flashback of sorts, Jesus will chide the arresting party by saying that they never tried to seize him when he was daily among them while teaching in the temple (14.49), that is, when he was openly with the Galilean crowds. Thus, Jesus' role as a teacher in these latter scenes is also critical for Mark, whether Mark conveys Jesus' teaching through depictions of his seated posture (12.41; 13.3) or through the actual teaching content itself.

From virtually the beginning to virtually the end of the narrative, then, Mark depicts Jesus as a teacher. That depiction occurs sometimes in narrated scenes, as again, for example, in 1.21-28, or in a lengthy litany of parables, as in 4.1-34 (cf. 4.1-2). At other times, Markan summaries also acknowledge Jesus' teaching (2.13; 6.6b). Furthermore, Jesus can teach anywhere: in synagogues (1.21-28; 6.2); near the 'sea' (or near an in-land lake, 2.13; 4.1); in various villages (6.6b); in the wilderness (6.34; cf. 6.31); and, at length, in the temple (12.35; cf. 14.49). Some of Jesus' most solemn and bold statements, moreover, are offered in a teaching context, as with, for example, his predictions about his forthcoming death and resurrection (8.31; cf. 9.31). So, 'teacher' is not an inadequate expression for Mark's view of Jesus.

Types of Teachers/Philosophers in the Ancient Mediterranean
Yet, what kind of teacher was the Markan Jesus? A simple presentation of Jesus as a teacher would not necessarily inspire followers because since

the classical period of Greek history some ancient Mediterranean thinkers resisted the title 'teacher' as too closely aligned with profiteering, a characteristic that Plato, Xenophon and Aristotle, for example, had welded to the term *Sophist*. As best we can tell, though, the first Sophists, fifth-century BCE teachers of rhetoric or the art of persuasion, were welcomed by most members of Athens's then newly emerging democracy. The Sophists taught everyday citizens how to defend a thesis in the open democratic space of debate. Furthermore, the Sophists appear to have been a part of a long-standing Panhellenic wisdom tradition, one that evolved from the so-called Seven Sages (Solon and Thales, among others) and the later Pre-Socratics, two groups of mostly itinerant intellectuals (in and beyond Athens) who served as 'publicly sanctioned mediators and legal experts' to insure concord within or among the ancient city-states (Tell 2011: 85, 93-112). As itinerant sages, the Sophists participated in diplomatic or inter-poleis (city-state) relations and gift exchanges, stayed as guests in the homes of the wealthy, and gained knowledge through their travels (as the character Odysseus did through his wanderings in the *Odyssey* [Tell 2011: 108-12]).

Plato, though, vehemently resisted describing Socrates as a teacher. Plato's Socrates avers that he 'has never been anyone's teacher' (Plato, *Apology* 33; cf. 19d; Xenophon, *Memorabilia* 1.6.13; cf. Epictetus, *Discourses* 3.5.17; 3.23.22), and Xenophon hesitates directly to attribute the label to Socrates (cf. Xenophon, *Memorabilia* 1.3-4). The Platonic Socrates' denial of the role is likely a factor of Plato's desire to distinguish Socrates from the Sophists whom Plato polemically brands as paid professionals. Thus, Socrates is not a teacher if the term means a 'fee-based' supervisor or someone contractually obligated to teach and offer an inculcative pedagogy (Scott 2000: 15-40). Such teachers, from Plato's perspective, are 'pastry chefs [and] flatterers' (*Gorgias*, 465a), pandering to their customers. By contrast, Socrates, who does not teach for a fee (Diogenes Laertius, *Lives of Eminent Philosophers* 2.5.27), challenges his auditors and interlocutors, produces aporia (i.e. perplexity or an unresolvable tension of thought) in the minds of his interlocutors by unsettling their prevailing notions of truth, and seeks truth through dialogue (Scott 2000: 44).

So, Plato's perspective, one which Xenophon and Aristotle likely shared, had the ultimate aim of discrediting the Sophists and undermining their authority (Tell 2011: 59) while lauding Socrates. Plato's view of the art of rhetoric as espoused by the Sophists (and apart from its use toward a philosophical end as he puts it in *Phaedrus*), moreover, was that rhetoric was deceptive and contingent speech intended to flatter the masses, not to achieve foundational truth. Such Sophists then in Plato's reckoning marketed wisdom (as opposed to receiving gifts simply for the wisdom they shared as a part of their diplomatic missions). In contrast to the description of the Sophists, Plato depicted Socrates as one who sought truth, one who did not pander to the crowds to gain esteem from them, and certainly not as one who charged fees for his professional services. In time, the defamation of the Sophists was folded into the emerging canons of invective or harshly critical literature. Vituperative or sharply critical characterizations of the Sophists or teachers then assisted one group to undermine the authority of yet another group.

So, again, what kind of teacher was Jesus? This was a real concern in the Markan age that inherited the virulent speech against the Sophists. How, as a sage, therefore, would Jesus have been perceived within the larger competitive cultures of philosophical movements? Furthermore, given the ignominious nature of his death by crucifixion, what would have been the perception of others about him and his successors? To what extent, moreover, is the Gospel of Mark a response to possible social critiques of Jesus' life as a teacher and of his movement?

It should be known that Christianity—like other philosophical groups—deployed conventional forms of polemical abuse and slander to vie against other philosophical movements both within and outside of Judaism (Johnson 1989: 429). Such philosophical movements slandered perceived rivals for what appeared to be excesses or deviance as if only *their own adherents* offered the route to achieve virtue. A rival was branded with a variety of caricatures such as a Sophist (*sophistēs*), a charlatan (*goēs*), or a brigand/usurper (*lēstēs*), all of which were vituperative descriptions of false philosophers.

Thus, in his characterization of Moses, for example, Philo of Alexandria critiqued the so-called Egyptian Sophists for their deceptions (*apatai*, *The Worse Attacks the Better*, 38.3). Responding to an attack on the Jews by Apion and other Alexandrians, Josephus lambastes Apion as a 'charlatan' (*Against Apion*, 2.1.3), the very label Apion had used to describe Moses (*Against Apion*, 2.14.145; 2.16.161; cf. Johnson 1989: 434-35).

Yet, Josephus would also use the negative label 'charlatan' to describe Justus of Tiberias, a Jew whose review of one of Josephus's writings Josephus had found wanting (*Life* 9.40; cf. Johnson 1989: 436). Josephus casts Judas the Galilean (who resisted Roman annexation) as a Sophist (*Jewish War* 2.118; cf. Johnson 1989: 436), while he viewed the Sicarii (whom Josephus mentions in association with the governorship of Felix [52–59 CE]) as brigands or usurpers (*lēstai, Jewish War* 2.8.6 .284; cf. Johnson 1989: 436), a vituperative expression that Josephus used to describe a variety of movements before and during the Jewish War (Grünewald 2004: 93-94; Marcus 1992: 449). Associates of Judas of Galilee, the Sicarii, and the other movements might have viewed such figures as persons resisting Roman domination or the infrastructure of provincial collaboration that supported it. All such brigands, in Josephus's eyes, though, were 'deceivers'. They 'deceived' (*apataō*) crowds (*Jewish Antiquities* 20.161). As 'deceivers' (*apateōnes*), they are paired with 'charlatans' (*goētes*, *Jewish Antiqui-ties* 20.167). One such brigand is described as a 'charlatan' (*goētos*) who deceived others by promising them salvation if they followed him into the wilderness (*Jewish Antiquities* 20.190). Josephus goes on to say that Gov-ernor Festus dispatched a force that destroyed both 'the [aforementioned] deceiver himself and those who had followed him' (*ton apatēsanta kai tous akolouthēsantas*, *Jewish Antiquities* 20.190).

Much earlier, as aforementioned, Plato, Xenophon and Aristotle had excoriated the first Sophists. For Plato, the Sophists were deceptive (Plato, *Apology* 18b, 19b-c) or were motivated by greed (Plato, *Hippias Major*, 282c-d). Moving about from city to city, they merchandize the soul (Plato, *The Sophists*, 224a-b; cf. Plato, *Timaeus*, 19e). In his work *On Hunting*, Xenophon devotes his last of thirteen chapters to a scathing critique of the Sophists. His standard polemics, which are intended to highlight the virtues of true philosophers, condemn the Sophists for their greed and guile. Osten-sibly, the Sophists should be 'leading' (*agõn*) others to virtue (13.1), but they teach bad or evil things (13.2). Their goal is their 'greed' (*pleonexia*, 13.10; 13.15) or 'gain' (*kerdos*, 13.8). Their guile is visible in their use of the art of 'deception' (*exapataõ*, 13.4; 13.8). For his part, Aristotle also casts the Sophist as a charlatan, 'one who makes money from an apparent but unreal wisdom' (*Sophistical Refutations*, 165a; cf. *Metaphysics*, 1004b).

Much later, particularly when speaking about the Sophist type, writers continued their denunciation of such teachers' dispositions. In the *Cynic Epistles* (likely from the first century CE), the character 'Socrates' speaks of Sophists who 'make money from philosophy' (*Of Socrates*, 1.10-11) and 'sell themselves for profit' (*kerdos*, *Socrates*, 1.5.7). In the *Orationes*, Dio Chrysostom avers that the ideal philosopher is a man 'without guile (*adolos*), speaking boldly (*parrēsiazomai*)... not for glory (*doxa*)... nor for money (*argyrion*)' in contrast to the Sophists (*sophistai*, 32.11) who offer set speeches for 'gain' (*kerdos*) and 'glory' (*doxa*, 32.10). Furthermore, while Dio refrains from seeing himself as a teacher (in a manner similar to Plato's Socrates; *Orationes*, 12.13), he also avers that he does not seek to 'deceive' (*exapataõ*, *Orationes*, 61.38). In *Alexander the False Prophet*, Lucian avers that Alexander joined up with a Byzantine musician and the two were partners in 'charlatanism (*goēteuõ*) and sorcery' (6.8). Further-more, in comparing Alexander to another brigand, Lucian states that Alex-ander was a 'more vicious usurper (*lēstēs*, 2.15-16) who did not simply infest (*lēsteuõ*, 2.18) a few places but has filled the whole Roman empire with his usurpation (*lēsteia*, 2.22)'. Again, such labels then were contemp-tuous and designed to commend one philosophical position just as much as they were intended to denounce other groups.

In contrast to the true philosopher, then, the charlatan/Sophist/brigand types were false philosophers (or leaders), false prophets, or false holy men. They were ignorant of true knowledge, purveyors of novelty (which was perennially deemed as subversive in ancient cultures), persons who preyed upon gullible crowds composed largely of those deemed to be the rabble rousers and uneducated audiences of the day. They gave persuasive speeches for profit, craved public acclaim and often looked for opportunities to display their beneficence or wonder-working powers to impress others. In the case of Peregrinus (a notorious charlatan type mentioned by the satirist Lucian of Samosata in Commagene), Peregrinus would take on one guise or another—a Cynic, a Christian, or an Egyptian ascetic who was willing even to imitate Hercules through self-immolation on a pyre at Olympia—for the sake of glory (Lucian, *Death of Peregrinus*, 1.3-4). More compactly, it could be said, then, that the charlatans, Sophists, and brigands, as they were caricatured, advocated gain, guile, and glory.

The Markan Jesus Grading Gain, Guile, and Glory

This social context in which virulent language was used against rival philosophical groups could explain then the Markan narrative's efforts to characterize Jesus as a teacher who did not seek gain, promote guile, or look for glory.

Against Gain

As aforementioned, seeking gain (*kerdos*) was one of the polemical charges lodged against ancient hucksters. From the vantage point of the teacher Jesus, 'to gain (*kerdainō*) the whole world was to lose one's soul or life' (8.36). That vantage point became clear in a teaching context (8.31-38) replete with 'soul' or 'life' (*psychē*) matters (8.35 [twice], 36, 37). Shortly before this context, Peter had identified Jesus as the Christ (8.30). When Jesus boldly (*parrhēsia*, 8.32) began to teach that his future would entail suffering, Peter did not hesitate to raise an objection. Peter's problem was his perspective, his way of 'thinking' (*phroneō*, 8.33). So, in this teaching context, Jesus shows his disciples how they must think to be prepared to follow him, to be able to take up a cross. His disciples must have the perspective of the things of God, not the things of human beings (8.33).

That perspective, moreover, widens one's vantage point to be able to grade soul matters apart from the conventional ledger system of this generation (8.38). This generation's limited perspective seeks to save life because it cannot see life from the chronological perspective of the coming Son of the Human One (aka. Son of Man) who, as the Gospel will reveal, will come with power when God's rule is fully consummated (8.38; 9.1; 13.26; 14.62). To think about soul or life matters without this wider vantage point then is to seek to save life in the face of crucibles, intense moments associated with shame. To think about soul or life matters without this wider vantage point is to misunderstand Jesus' role as the Christ as if the role elevates his status in the conventional currencies of thought. It does not. To think about soul or life matters without the wider vantage point is to be misled about what is valuable and what is not. While conventional currencies would place value in seeking to gain the whole world, Jesus does not grade seeking gain as an option for his disciples. Seeking gain is tied to an order of life or a world-view that is not informed by the economy of the fully consummated rule of God. What must shape the thinking of Jesus' disciples, then, is always a wider vantage point, a different way of thinking. Again, they must think from the wider vantage point of 'the things of God' (8.33).

This wider vantage point is on display again when Jesus the teacher (10.17, 20) meets a rich man who wants to inherit eternal life (10.17). While the man has kept multiple commandments since he was a youth, the one thing he lacked was a perspective on his possessions. He *has* possessions (10.21) and he *has* many of them (10.22). *Having* treasure in heaven (10.21) ultimately means that one has to have a different orientation to one's posses-sions, to see them as an opportunity to aid the poor (10.21), not to enhance one's standing before others. Thus, the seeker grievingly walks away from Jesus' invitation to discipleship (10.22). As Jesus reveals, the seeker's prob-lem, incorrectly evaluating one's possessions, is a concern for many people who have wealth (10.23). The wider evaluative perspective of the rule of God must shape one's attitude toward all of one's attachments—from things to family to land (10.28-31). So, turning from homes, family, and land, while good, is not sufficient unless it is done so for the sake of the gospel, which fundamentally asserts that the rule of God has both broken into the world and yet has not been fully consummated (cf. 1.14-15).

Against Guile

The teacher Jesus also critiques guile, another negative trait lodged against ancient hucksters. Guile (*apataō*) and wealth (*ploutos*) are brought together as Jesus explains the parable of the Sower (4.3-20). Told in a teaching con-text replete with parables (4.1-34), the Sower parable exposes the varying types of persons hearing the word. The four soils—ground along the way, rocky ground, thorny ground, and good ground—represent the quality of reception of the Sower's word. In the case of the thorny ground, some per-sons can hardly grow or produce fruit because their concerns—whether the cares for the world, the deceit of riches, or other desires—choke the word (4.19).

In yet another instance, Jesus also teaches against guile and gain together. That is, in a teaching context on 'heart' (*kardia*) matters (7.1-23, esp. vv. 6, 19, 21), Jesus places guile (rendered this time as the Greek word *dolos*) and greed (*pleonexia*) in a long vice list of traits that his disciples must avoid (7.21-23). While Jesus' stylized opponents are preoccupied with externals such as washing hands before eating (7.1-2), Jesus internalizes ethics with his focus on the 'heart'. A heart ethic then upholds the traditions of God over the traditions of human beings (7.8-13). A heart ethic also places the origin of defilement not on the outside but on the inside (7.14-23).

Such internal vices as guile and greed then expose a heart that is defiled, which the Gospel will confirm in its closing scenes when the Sanhedrin authorities (chief priests and scribes), as Mark has stylized them, will 'seek out' (*zēteō*, 14.1) a way to arrest Jesus by 'stealth' (by 'guile' as noted by the Greek word *dolos*), while one of Jesus' twelve disciples will 'seek' (*zēteō*) an opportunity (*eukairōs*, 14.11) to hand Jesus over to the Sanhedrin for money.

Against the Quest for Glory (or Selfish Ambition)
The Markan Jesus clearly also critiqued the quest for glory. His posture of prayer (1.35; cf. 6.41; 8.6; 14.22) deflected honor away from himself and toward the deity (Struthers Malbon 2009: 133). His inclusion of a wide variety of dining partners also went against the grain of prevailing practices that supported a quest for fame and its enhancement through a calibrated selection of one's commensal and traveling company. Furthermore, in two teaching contexts (9.31-37; 10.35-45) along his journey he challenged his disciples not to 'desire' (*thelō*) to be first (9.35; 10.44) or to be the greatest (9.34; 10.43) as reckoned in the conventional order. In yet another teaching context (12.38-40), the Markan Jesus castigated the 'desires' (*thelō*, 12.38) of the scribes (again as the Gospel stylizes some of them), for such scribes were giving the appearance of piety but in fact were fame seekers and devourers of the homes of widows.

Conceivably, then, Mark was written to dispel some of the lethal polemics volleyed against Christianity as a philosophical movement. Certainly by the second century CE, Christianity's critics from Celsus to Lucian perceived Christianity as a collection of charlatans. As noted by Origen (Origen, *Against Celsus*, 1.71; II.62-68), Celsus, for example, described Jesus as an itinerant charlatan (*goēs*) working among the ignorant and his followers as persons drawn from the lower classes. Lucian described Christians as persons who 'scorn death' (*Death of Peregrinus*, 13) and Jesus as a 'crucified Sophist' (literally, 'a Sophist fixed on a pole'; *Death of Peregrinus*, 13).

There is reason to believe, though, that even in the first century CE similar perceptions of Christianity were already evident, especially because of the ignominious way in which Jesus died, that is, by crucifixion. Thus, Paul looks out on the bleak landscape of a 'cross' logic and calls Jesus' crucifixion 'a stumbling block to the Jews and foolishness to the Greeks' (1 Cor. 1.23). Yet, Paul reframes the despised Christ Jesus as wisdom (1.30). Sensing the humiliation associated with crosses, the writer of Hebrews speaks of Jesus as having 'endured the cross, disregarding its shame' and reframes

Jesus' present position as one who has been elevated to be seated at the right hand of the throne of God (Heb. 12.2). While some of the charges against Christianity dripped with more hyperbole than truth, it is reasonable to assume that Christianity was castigated as 'a lower class movement... as uneducated and socially insignificant, if not downright irresponsible or dangerous' (Malherbe 1985: 196). As with Paul and with the later writer of Hebrews, then, Jesus' followers re-framed the position of an otherwise despised leader from the perspective of the Romans who put him to death.

Living in a world where perception of others always mattered (Lendon 1997: 37), how could the Markan author—like other early Christians—rehabilitate the image of Jesus after he had suffered such public humiliation as a whipped and crucified leader? This matter of perception was likely an important issue for Mark's earliest auditors. When the arresting rabble seizes Jesus at night in Gethsemane, for example, Jesus chafes that he is treated as a brigand or usurper (14.48), for which death by a cross would be expected (cf. 15.27). Not long after his disciples learn that they must take up their cross and follow Jesus, he warns them not to be ashamed of him and of his words lest in turn he is ashamed of them in an ultimate court of prestige from which they needed to gain a sense of perspective (8.38). Scattered throughout the Gospel of Mark, moreover, are explicit and implicit queries about the social identity of Jesus or the nature of his work, as if such concerns about perception were pivotal for understanding the logic of Mark's Gospel. Such questions included the following:

> 'What is this? A new teaching?' (1.27)
> 'Why does this one speak thus?... Who is able to release sins except God?' (2.7)
> 'Who then is this...?' (4.41)
> 'From where did this one [get] these things? And who gave this one wisdom? And what are such powers coming about through his hands?' (6.2)
> 'Who do the people say me to be?' (8.27)
> 'But who do you say me to be?' (8.29)
> 'Good teacher, what must I do to inherit eternal life?' (10.17)
> 'By what authority are you (singular) doing these things?' Or 'Who gave you this authority that you might do these things?' (11.28)
> 'As against a brigand or usurper, did you come out with swords and clubs to arrest me?' (14.48)
> 'Are you the Christ, the Son of the Blessed?' (14.61)
> 'Are you the King of the Judeans' (15.2)

All such questions likely engaged the imaginations of the earliest auditors in a story seeking to clarify and re-frame the identity of a despised Jesus if not also to rehabilitate an image of his followers in a social context awash with the 'fierce disputation' of rival, competing philosophical movements (Johnson 1989: 29). If the Markan Gospel—with other Christian writings of the time—is concerned about explaining Jesus' ignominious death, such aforementioned questions could also seek to legitimate Jesus in a world in which other wonder-workers were polemicized as charlatans. In that sense, then, the Gospel of Mark is a story *about* Jesus, a story seeking to distinguish him from others whose powerful works were deemed as the disingenuous acts of self-interested deviants. Yet, for those who first heard the Gospel, it was also a Gospel *for* them. As they were being hustled up on trumped up charges, the Gospel's rehabilitated image of Jesus provided inspiration for them as well. The Gospel's story of Jesus the teacher thus supplied them with abiding values that would help them endure their own shame-ridden crucible moments (13.9-13).

Chapter Outline

Thus, the argument presented here about Mark's characterization of Jesus will develop in five chapters along with a conclusion. Chapter 1, 'Mark as a *Life* about Jesus', will argue that Mark is an ancient biography or *Life* (*bios* in Greek). Initially, the chapter makes a case for Mark as a biography despite the reticence of many contemporary scholars to see the ancient *Life* as Mark's generic prototype. That is, the chapter will argue that the Markan author deployed the conventions of a specific subtype of the ancient biography, namely, the *professional* biography. Furthermore, the chapter will argue that as a professional biography, the Gospel of Mark told a story *about* the adult professional work of Jesus the teacher. To dispel possible negative perceptions about an otherwise despised Jesus, particularly about the teacher's death, Mark's professional biography likely deployed *general* rhetorical strategies customarily used to enhance the image of a person in the ancient world. Next, Chapter 2, 'Mark as a *Life* for Others', will argue that the Markan professional biography could have been heard as a story acoustically arranged with multiple repetitive patterns about Jesus' preparation of his followers. Thus, while the story is about Jesus, its impact is not to produce an abstract treatise or Christology about Jesus. Rather, the story was likely arranged rhetorically to offer inspirational assistance to Mark's earliest auditors as they faced the catalogue of hardships listed in Mk 13.9-13. Then, in the remaining three chapters, the textbook turns to three *specific* characterization typologies that would likely have provided symbolic social capital for Mark's rehabilitation of the image of Jesus. Thus, Chapter 3, 'Mark as a Prophetic Envoy', will argue that the Gospel of Mark portrays Jesus as both a prophet and an envoy. While Mark presents Jesus' death as a consequence of a choice that Jesus makes (St Clair 2008: 111-27), Mark deploys the prophetic envoy typology to recast the ignominy of Jesus' death as inevitable and tragic. Mark does not shy away from the shame of the cross. Blood spilled is blood shown. Yet, Mark insists that what happened to the crucified teacher should not be seen as failure. Rather, as a prophetic envoy sent by the deity, Jesus actually deserved honor, the requisite honor due to the deity sending him. Mark depicts Jesus' death then as an affront to the deity and that affront as a turning point in the Gospel's chronological timetable for the final stages of God's ongoing intervention in the world. Chapter 4 will argue that Mark also presents 'Jesus as a Powerful Broker'. If the crucifixion of Jesus makes it appear that he died as a powerless victim, the whole of the Gospel positions him as a man of power, a mediating figure whose Septuagint-based brokerage style stands in contrast to the brokerage patterns of Rome's representatives. Then, Chapter 5 will argue that Mark also presents 'Jesus as a Philosophical Hero' even as he moves toward death's doors. As with the Markan author's contemporaries, the author of Mark did not embrace the Socratic version of the philosophical hero without adjustments. Like such contemporaries, the Markan author did not seek to sanitize the death of Jesus. Rather, in rich detail, the Gospel of Mark seeks to show the struggles of a heroic Jesus as he moved toward a resolute stance in the face of a shame-ridden crucible. Such a picture of struggle likely gave succor to Mark's earliest auditors as they themselves tried heroically to face a litany of shame-filled moments before tyranny's representatives as well.

While the three typologies rehabilitated the image of Jesus, they also provided values by which Mark's earliest auditors could order their lives. Such auditors could see themselves as prophetic envoys, deserving better than they received; as powerful brokers, proclaiming the Gospel to the nations; and as philosophical heroes, facing death with valor. So, the Markan story was not solely *about* Jesus. It was also *for* his followers. The typologies altogether also revealed what the Gospel was *against*. Mark's narrative tells a story about a clash between the use of power to do good and the use of power to humiliate and abuse those who are already aggrieved.

Finally, in the Conclusion, questions are raised about the ethics of Mark's Gospel in today's world. What are the benefits of Mark's rehabilitated images of Jesus? What are some of the limitations of Mark's typological presentation of Jesus as a teacher? Can the anticipated rest of the good news that the Gospel begins turn the Gospel's proposed ideology against itself?

Chapter 1

MARK AS A *LIFE* ABOUT JESUS

Introduction

This chapter argues that Mark is a biography *about* Jesus. For many scholars, Mark's Gospel certainly does not have the structure, substance, or style deemed requisite for the prototypical biography of the ancient world. As we shall see, however, ancient biographies had subtypes and Mark resonates well with one of those subtypes, the professional biography. As a professional biography about Jesus that deploys a popular style, Mark tells a basic story about Jesus as a teacher even as it deploys specific rhetorical strategies often used to rehabilitate tarnished images in Mark's world. This chapter thus will clarify how Mark's biography deployed those strategies to respond to some of the negative criticism that early Christianity's opponents could have had about Jesus as a teacher, especially the key negative criticism about the shameful nature of Jesus's death on a cross. Ideologically, then, Mark's story about Jesus reshapes the image of Jesus so that the close of his adult ministry would not have seemed as a failure.

Scholarly Reticence to Read Mark as a Biography

Many scholars suggest that all of the canonical Gospels were written at a popular level and thus it would be a mistake to think that these narratives matched the style and artistic craft of biographical works written by Suetonius (late first century CE) and Plutarch (early second century CE). In fact, the closest that these Gospels come to exhibiting a biographical literary flair may be seen in the so-called passion anecdotes, which seem more tightly woven and dramatically artful. The failure of all the Gospels to write with such an assumed literary flair—including Luke who is sometimes seen as a *litterateur* by comparison to the other Synoptics (Matthew and Mark)—is one of the main reasons that some (form critical and redaction critical) scholars—over a period of about 125 years—looked elsewhere beyond the ancient *bios* (biography or 'life') to find a genre prototype for the Gospels (Burridge 2004: 24).

Many form critics (who were interested in the oral transmission of gospel traditions) argued that the canonical Gospels were *sui generis*, that is, unique collections of cultic folktales that indicated the consciousness of cultic communities but not the type of creativity of individual authors that these scholars attributed to the contemporary counterparts of the Gospels (Talbert 1977; Burridge 2004: 7-13). Thus, form critics assumed that the Gospels could not be compared to ancient biographies or to any works in their literary environment. Redaction critics (who were interested in the creativity of the Evangelists or the individual authors behind the Gospels) did not view the Evangelists as mindless editors artlessly and haphazardly stringing together collections of community tales but many a redaction critic also held on to the idea that the Gospels were unique. In all earnestness, though, this view of the Gospel genre or of any genre as unique is theoretically implausible. As Christopher Bryan has asserted, 'the notion of a writer proceeding without genre, or creating a totally new genre (*sui generis*), is (even if theoretically possible) akin to the notion of a writer choosing to write in an unknown language... In fact, the wildest artistic experimentation invariably has some connection, either by adaptation or reaction, to what has preceded it' (1993: 12).

Still, some scholars may object to the ancient *bios* as the *particular* genre that best captures the content and form of the canonical Gospels because the Gospels are not structured with the same chronological or topical interests. Furthermore, the Gospels are not written with the same sophisticated narrative prose of many of the well-known biographies of the period.

Mark as a Professional Biography

In response, it must be stated that genres of any period are flexible sets of conventions shared by authors and audiences, not rigid, prescriptive Procrustean beds (Burridge 2004: 32, 43-47, 77). Furthermore, there is sufficient evidence to show that biographies of the period were themselves diverse, if not at times complex. Some were 'full' biographies, structured to cover a variety of topics from the heroic person's *genos* (ancestors), birth, childhood, and mature years to his or her death. The biographies of Plutarch and Suetonius, for example, illustrate this type (Hägg 2012: 99-100), though Plutarch had a stronger interest in chronology than Suetonius did. Similarly, the pseudo-Herodotean biography of Homer exploits the 'full' type. That is, it recounts Homer's life from birth to death, his epigrams (or terse and witty sayings), and his travels to various cities that acted inhospitably toward him (Compton 2006: 70-71). By contrast, some other biographies were 'professional', meaning that they only depicted a subject's adult or 'professional' life, as with the *Life of Aesop* (Hägg 2012: 99, 102).

If ancient authors and auditors knew that biographies could be full or professional, they also knew that biographies could be *refined* or *popular*. Again, the biographies of Plutarch and Suetonius were viewed as aesthetically refined biographies of the period, though both used a simple style (Burridge 2004: 176). While the pseudo-Herodotean biography of Homer was also a 'full' biography, it was written on a popular style, without literary pretensions. Among the professional lives, the *Life of Aesop* was also written at this popular level. Such popular Greek works deployed Koine (common, marketplace) Greek, a simple vocabulary, and a paratactic style (literally meaning a side-by-side ordering of episodes), with a relative preference for coordinating conjunctions such as *kai* ('and'), as opposed to the subordinating conjunctions that characterized the more refined prose of the day (Tolbert 1996: 68). Examinations of the Gospels, then, must take into consideration the full-versus-professional or refined-versus-popular polarities on which biographical frameworks could be developed, along with other similarities and differences that obtained between the canonical Gospels on the one hand and the other works typically known as ancient biographies on the other.

Accordingly, while all of the canonical Gospels were popular, both the Gospel of Matthew and the Gospel of Luke appear to have drawn on the conventions of the 'full' biography in their portraits of Jesus as a rejected prophet. That is, they show an interest in the ancestry of Jesus (Mt. 1.2-17; Lk. 3.23-38) and in his birth and childhood (Mt. 1.18–2.23; Lk. 1.5–2.52) along with his adult ministry and death. Given Luke's use of the rhetorical device of synkrisis (detailed comparison) in reference to John and Jesus, it appears that Luke also drew on the 'full' biographical format to depict the beginning, adult career, and prophetic end of the life of John the Baptist. For both Matthew and Luke, however, gaps remained, with each narrative offering 'emblematic scenes', that is, scenes that economically reproduced the essence of a life in a limited medium (Hägg 2012: 7)—such as Mt. 2.1-23 (on the continuing vulnerability of Jesus as Messiah) and Lk. 2.40-52 (on the wisdom of Jesus).

By contrast, the Gospel of Mark appears to be a popular, 'professional' biography, while the Gospel of John, ever the different Gospel compared to the Synoptics, is a hybrid. Like Mark, John has no interest in speaking explicitly about the birth and formative childhood experiences of Jesus as a rejected prophet. Like Matthew and Luke, John is not satisfied strictly with a 'professional' biography. That is, John's prologue speaks of the *logos* (or 'word') as an agent of creation on the order of Personified Wisdom (as in Prov. 8.1-31 and Sir. 24.3-8). Thus, for John, long before the 'word' became flesh and was rejected, it had already been the primary agent through which the created order had come into being.

If such readings of the canonical Gospels are correct, Mark is a biography despite its differences from Matthew and Luke, that is, despite its lack
of an interest in the ancestry or early formative period of Jesus' life (Perkins
2007: 23). In fact, if one assumes the Markan Priority hypothesis (again,
that Mark was written first and Matthew and Luke drew on Mark), the revi-
sions that Matthew and Luke gave to Mark (which included 'such items as
genealogy, birth prodigies, and elements of chronology along with additional material about Jesus' teaching') likely indicate that 'the later Evangelists were filling out what they took to be a life of Jesus' (Perkins 2007:
127). That is, they read Mark as a biography and continued to develop stories about Jesus in the direction of what would have been deemed as *fuller*
subtypes of biographies. At the beginning of a narrative fount of collections
of tales about Jesus, Mark thus is an innovative biographical work, 'the earliest written narrative to combine an account of Jesus' ministry with a report
about his final days in Jerusalem' (Perkins 2007: 126).

Seeing the canonical Gospels—including Mark—as 'a subcategory of
the ancient literary genre "life"' (Perkins 2007: 3) need not suggest that no
differences obtained between the canonical Gospels and other ancient biographies. Ancient readers or auditors unfamiliar with Israel's descendants
or with Christianity, for example, might find in the canonical Gospels an
'obscure' subject, 'a thin chronology', a short scope for the subject's life
(given the primary interest that these Gospels place on Jesus' last days),
with little, if any, evaluation of the subject's deeds and teachings, and little,
if any, authorial self-identification (Perkins 2007: 3-11).

Still, as Hägg has noted, both subtypes share 'the anonymity [of the
author], the episodic structure, the peripateticism [i.e. virtually all the
famous subjects travel from place to place], the different combination and
interpretation of common biographical elements, and the unhappy end of
life (though in the case of the gospels profoundly reversed through the resurrection)' (2012: 147). Both also deploy their own distinctive 'cultural
archetypes' and present their subjects with a fairly 'fixed' and ideal character (Perkins 2007: 3, 7, 9). Both use summaries and collections of sayings to
demonstrate the essence of a subject's life (Perkins 2007: 4-5). Both deploy
episodes from the subject's life to illustrate the subject's message and to
demonstrate the essence of the subject's life from birth to death (or a sub-
stantial part of it [Perkins 2007: 3]).

Furthermore, while the Gospels rarely provide any direct evaluation of
their subject's life, the net effect of an evaluation still occurs through the
Gospel's use of cultural archetypes from Israel's scriptures to define the
overall character of Jesus and through a protracted account of Jesus' final
days to depict the innocent suffering of Jesus (Perkins 2007: 7). Indeed,
what distinguishes the Gospels from other ancient biographies may be two
factors: (1) the nuancing of the Gospels to align them with the 'biographical

elements in the Jewish Scriptures'; and (2) the brevity of Jesus' life, which thus does not allow for much of a focus on Jesus' life (Perkins 2007: 11).

Mark as a Biography with a Popular Style

Mark is not a sophisticated narrative. 'Prolix', 'verbose', 'awkward', and 'clumsy': these are just a few of the adjectives once used to describe Mark (Johnson 1986: 150; Stanton 1992: 326; Farmer 1964: 122). As Etienne Trocmé once stated, 'the author of Mark was a clumsy writer unworthy of mention in any history of literature' (1975: 73). Why were such views once voiced about Mark's Gospel? In part, the negative assessment of Mark's style was based on the Gospel's proclivity for repetition, as in, for example, the Gospel's pleonastic or wordy temporal expressions, multiple triads, and intercalations. That is, the Gospel deploys repetitive temporal expressions such as 'when it was evening, after the sun set' (1.32) or 'on that day, when evening had come' (4.35) or 'on this very night, before the cock crows twice' (14.30). Likewise, the Gospel has a love for threes, as in the case of its three passion/resurrection prediction patterns (8.31-32; 9.31-32; 10.32-33). The Gospel also has a fondness for 'compound verbs followed by the same preposition (1.16; 10.25; 15.32)', two-step progressions or explanatory appositions (1.32; 4.35; 9.3), and intercalations or a-b-a collections of alternating episodes (5.21-24a/5.25b-34/5.35-43; 6.6b-13/6.14-29/6.30; 11.12-14/11.15-18/11.20-25) though scholars debate the appropriate terminology (inclusios or 'sandwiches') for such units and the number of intercalations that the Gospel actually includes (Kelber 1983: 64-67).

In truth, all writings of the period deployed repetition. That is, repetition is a necessity in any cultural context of 'widespread [reading and writing] illiteracy', where both the leisure to study and its access were limited to the elite or those controlled by the elite (Keith 2011: 71-123). Mark's cultural context is one in which persons could have been 'textually adept without being textually literate' (Keith 2011: x). Given this kind of illiteracy, most persons would have heard texts but they would not have been able to read them. Spoken or written forms of communication thus required repetition to help auditors make sense of what they heard. So, from Homer's multiple stereotyped scenes (such as guest-reception scenes and recognition scenes [scenes in which the true identity and status of characters are revealed]) in Greek to Seneca's symmetry and Pliny's parallels in Latin, all writers from the period reveled in repetition.

Accordingly, while Mark's Koine Greek and its limited vocabulary of about 1,270 words in an approximate overall count of 11,242 words distinguished the Gospel from those first-century texts that approximated elite Attic prose and while Mark's paratactic style may indicate a general, popular style if not also some Semitic influence (such as was the case with the

Greek of the Septuagint), neither popular nor elite works of the period could afford to avoid some level of repetition (Wegener 1995: 4; Burridge 2004: 194). Repetition aided the auditors' organization and amplification of a narrative (Welch 1981: 8-15, Notopoulos 1951; cf. *Rhetorica ad Herennium*, 4.42.54-56; Cicero, *De oratore*, 63.212; Dionysius of Halicarnassus, *Demosthenes*, 48), as such narratives were performed and likely improvised. Unlike modern writings, in which repetition is often avoided, ancient writings included repetitive composition as a fundamental given with occasional digressions to shift a narrative's focus or break its pace while yet maintaining an overall synthesis or organic unity (Longinus, *Sublime*, 40.2; Dionysius of Halicarnassus, *On Word Arrangement*, 3; Freudenburg 1993: 132-73). Repetition, then, need not indicate a lack of skill but rather the artfulness of a writer who needed to emphasize a point for a listening audience (Shiner 1998: 169).

In part, moreover, Mark often yields a negative assessment from interpreters simply because it deploys a popular style. Evaluations of Mark as clumsy or verbose, then, are remarkably similar to the ones once made about other popular works, namely, the *Life of Aesop*, the Pseudo-Herodotean *Life of Homer*, and *An Ephesian Tale* (also known as *Ephesiaca*). The *Life of Aesop* was once critiqued, for example, as 'clumsy patchwork', a 'cut-and-paste job', and 'lacking in any underlying pattern or structure' (Holzberg 1993: 77-78). *The Life of Homer* certainly was once considered little more than a satirical pastiche that few elites would have harbored seriously (cf. Hägg 2012: 135, 141). Likewise, according to Richard Pervo, 'at first reading... [*An Ephesian Tale*] appears to lack sophistication or subtlety of plot, style, theme, or characterization' (2008: 70). For all of these other popular narratives, though, the tide has now turned with many critics beginning to measure these texts by their own aesthetic qualities: for example, their use of epigrams, fables, or poetic verses to provide commentary on the drive of the larger narrative; or their deployment of reduplication, that is, the repetition of similar episodes, which help to organize the episodic structure of the story. So, while the *Life of Aesop* and the *Life of Homer* were written in everyday Koine and *Ephesiaca* in a type of Attic (or classical) Greek influenced by Koine, the aforementioned motifs still point to the creative control of an author (cf. Tolbert 1996: 68).

Accordingly, in the *Life of Aesop*, Aesop tells maxims and fables that comment on the rest of the narrative. In his defense, for example, Aesop relates the embedded tale of the frog whose murder of a mouse actually causes the frog's own death. That is, the frog fable is designed to speak about the larger story in which the death of Aesop eventuates in a plague on the Delphians, Aesop's false accusers (Compton 1990: 339). The many epigrams in the *Life of Homer* work similarly (Lefkowitz 1981: 21), as does the oracle of Apollo in *An Ephesian Tale* (1.5.6), which roughly adumbrates the plot's sequence. Thus, such smaller tales and poetic or proverbial verses reflect their respective author's or editor's overall sense of the plot (Hägg 2012: 135, 137; Tolbert 1996: 105).

Reduplication also pervades all three of these popular narratives. All deploy what Corinne Jouanno readily saw both in the *Life of Aesop* and the *Life of Alexander*, yet another popular *bios* of the period, namely, the 'principle of seriality' (Jouanno 2009: 38). With such a principle, 'more or less similar structures tend to recur again and again, and the very phenomenon of reduplication gives the whole work a kind of unity' (Jouanno 2009: 38). So, although Aesop is routinely mistreated in the *Life of Aesop*, he constantly solves enigmas for a master or a city. Similarly, upon Homer's arrival in different cities, he repeatedly takes a seat and performs his poetry (*Life of Homer* 2.9-10, 12, 15) while listening audiences repeatedly marvel at the blind bard's gift. Anthia and Habrocomes face similar, stereotyped ordeals such as crucifixions, shipwrecks, and incarceration. In the case of incarceration, their parallel ordeals are literally interlaced so that auditors are forced to follow the plot 'back and forth' in observing their similar struggles (Pervo 2008: 71).

Thus, Markan scholars have now begun to appreciate Mark's popular style. Scholars are not surprised about the Gospel's episodic structure, its paratactic style, its preference for the historical present (the use of the present tense verbal forms to speak more vividly about past occurrences, as in most of the mocking scene of 15.16-20), and various aforementioned repetitive features. These features need not indicate an awkward editor either unable or unwilling to stitch better seams between source and redactive material (Kelber 1983: 64-67; Wegener 1995: 4). Rather, Mark seems to deploy some of the same stylistic features that were deployed by the aforementioned works that drew on a popular style.

Read from within its own popular milieu, for example, Mark's second longest parable (the parable of the Tenants in Mark 12) is not odd in its placement outside of Mark's long parable collection in Mark 4. Both the parable of the Sower and the parable of the Tenants may be understood as embedded narratives that summarize features of the larger Markan plot. So, while Mark does not include fables as in the *Life of Aesop* or an onslaught of epigrams as in the *Life of Homer*, it does deploy these parables as summative commentaries on portions of the larger plot. So, in addition to the Gospel's short editorial summaries (*Sammelberichte*, e.g. 1.14-15; 1.32-34; 3.7-12; 6.54-56) deemed by an earlier generation as the seams through which a Markan editor wove together select sources and its analeptic actorial summaries such as the one given by the synagogue participants (6.1-2) or the one given by Peter (10.28), the Gospel also deploys two key parables that serve as plot synopses, namely, the parable of the Sower in Mark 4 and the parable of the Tenants in Mark 12 (Donahue 1973: 206-209). As Mary

Ann Tolbert has persuasively argued, these two parables reveal the basic principles underlying the whole gospel (Tolbert 1996: 103-106, 122, 151-52). Both parables are embedded tales about the receptions of other characters to the message and messengers sent to them by God. The parable of the Sower provides a basic typology of responses that other characters will make to the Sower. That is, what is said about the types of ground or soil in the Sower parable are symbolic cues of the various ways that characters in Mark's Gospel will respond to Jesus. Likewise, as Tolbert asserts, the parable of the Tenants is critical for the Gospel because it 'pictures the arrival and death of the heir of the vineyard' (1996: 122). That is, one part of the parable portrays Jesus as an esteemed emissary, one of several in a litany of 'four acts of sending' (Tolbert 1996: 235). A second part describes what the 'lord of the vineyard' (the very one who has carefully protected and cared for it, cf. Isa. 5.1-2) will do upon the murder of the last emissary, the vineyard owner's beloved son (Tolbert 1996: 237).

As we shall see in Chapter 3 of this Guide, the issue of 'reception', which is emphasized in both parables, is a critical theme in the Gospel. So, on the one hand, in the parable of the Sower, the 'reception' focus primarily features the reception of the Sower's word. If the disciples are the 'rocky' ground that receives the Sower's word, as Tolbert argues (1996: 156), for example, the parable's own commentary aptly describes the story line for the disciples. That is, they are not sufficiently rooted in the right values to face 'tribulation (or alienation) or persecution' (4.17). Thus, as the narrative progresses, Jesus repeatedly will model prophetic values with the goal of preparing the disciples for pressure-filled times. On the other hand, in the parable of the Tenants, a wider scope of the story world is provided, one that reveals how several messenger-brokers are received and the basis of their authority. Thus, the parable of the Tenants (or what could be called the parable of the Dishonored Emissaries) provides commentary on the back-story, the story, and the aftermath of the Gospel, as Diagram 1 illustrates.

Thus, Mark's story of Jesus as a teacher is a part of a larger story-world of rejection. For Mark, the death of the 'beloved son' and heir of the vineyard is not the end of the story. It is actually the beginning of the final series of the deity's liberative acts. The larger story world—through which Markan auditors must see their pressure-filled moments—is one for which the deity, then, has already acted and will continue to act beyond the closing events on the narrative stage. Understanding Mark's deployment of parables as embedded tales in accordance with the use of such tales in other popular narratives then does not reveal an author writing a disparate story. Rather, it reveals the Markan author's consistent judgment on the established order. Mark insists that the established order is constrained by the longer temporal order of the deity's liberative acts.

Diagram 1

| Parable of the Tenants (or the Parable of the Emissaries, Mark 12) | Plot Synopsis of the back-story, the persecution of God's prophets, and aftermath of the murder of the Vineyard Owner's Son |

God's care of the vineyard (12.1) (pre-narrative stage)   God sends prophets and a son; all are persecuted and the son is murdered (12.2-8)   God responds to the tenants' actions (12.9) (post-narrative stage)

Read from within its own popular milieu, Mark's repetitive string of parables in 4.1-34 and the string of miracles in 4.35–5.43 are not odd. Both strings follow the aforementioned principle of seriality often found in popular narratives. So, for example, the string of parables in 4.1-34 need not be considered an extraneous collection. Rather, given the abundance of acoustics diction found in 4.1-34 (see Diagram 2), the Gospel deploys the string—and especially the parable of the Sower—at the least to make comments on the quality of the hearing of the characters found elsewhere in the Gospel. For those who hear well and are receptive, fruitfulness follows and they do not fall away. For those who do not, failure follows with some even losing what they once had. In Mk 4.1-34, auditors learn on the one hand that the truth (or light) about the deity's dominion inevitably will be revealed (and thus cannot be hidden) and that it will ultimately succeed. On the other hand, auditors learn that the reception of truth depends on how well persons actually hear what is revealed. Thus, those who truly hear (those who act on what they have heard) can already begin to accrue the benefits of the deity's dominion.

Diagram 2
Akouō ('I hear') Diction in Mark 4.1-34

akouete ('listen', 4.3)
akouein akouetō ('[ears] to hear, let that one listen', 4.9)
akouontes akouōsin ('hearing, they may hear',4.12)
akousōsin ('they hear', 4.15, 16)
akousantes ('after hearing',4.18)
akouousin ('they hear', 4.20)
akouein akouetō ('[ears] to hear, let that one listen', 4.23)
akouete ('you [plural] hear', 4.24)
akouein ('to hear', 4.33)

Likewise, Mark's string of miracles in 4.35–5.43 is not odd. Rather, Mark deploys the string to reiterate a theme: Jesus' authority and ability to handle hostile take-overs. Accordingly, in his response to a chaotic sea, Jesus—as if to reenact a Mosaic miracle—demonstrates power over the sea. In fact, the diction of 1.21-28 prepares auditors to see the miracle at 'sea' in 4.35-41 as yet another example of Jesus' power over chaotic forces. That is, both miracles use rebuke diction (*epitimaō*, 1.25; 4.39), silence diction ('Be silent' [*phimoō*], 1.25; and 'Be still' [*phimoō*], 4.39); and the diction of obedience (*hypakouoō*, 1.27; 4.41). So, the miracle at 'sea' is not simply an account of Jesus' ability to protect his disciples. Rather, it is an example of power over a sea, which veritably re-enacts a tradition associated with the ancient prophetic broker Moses (cf. Struthers Malbon 2012: 483). Furthermore, in stilling the storm, Jesus produced a great (*megas*) calm to match the size of the great (*megas*) storm (4.35-41, esp. 4.37, 39). In his response to a demonic militia that reduced a man to incivility, Jesus brought serenity and sanity (5.1-20). In his response to an alienating force that had subjected a woman to an enslaving (whipping) affliction for twelve years, Jesus brought peace (5.25-34). When death had freshly robbed life from a twelve-year old girl, moreover, Jesus—like an Elijah or Elisha—freshly restored life to the child and the child to her parents (5.35-43). Thus, this string of miracles should remind auditors that Jesus' journey is one of deliverance on the order of the deity's acts of deliverance in the past. The present examples of such deliverance suggest that no hostile takeovers past or present are too 'great' or enduring for the deity that Jesus represents to overcome.

General Rhetorical Strategies in Mark's Life about Jesus

If a key goal of the Gospel of Mark as a story about Jesus was to rehabilitate Jesus' image as a teacher, what rhetorical public relations strategies were available? At least three rhetorical strategies were available to enhance the image of dramatis personae (or characters in a story) in the ancient world. Such strategies addressed the basic tripartite parts of a biography, namely, the beginning, middle, and end. These strategies, it should be stated, were not solely used to repair an image that had been tarnished. They also provided the basic rhetorical infrastructure for constructing *good lives* in the ancient world.

The Markan Teacher and the Rhetoric of Descent

First, a writer could deploy the rhetoric of 'descent' (Bernstein 2008: 10), which would show a character's distinction in association with his or her lineage or kin-group. In essence, the focus here is on a good entrance into life. Accordingly, the well-born touted their pedigree (as did Josephus in *Life* 1-8) or swapped genealogies in competitive exchanges (as did Glaucus and Diomedes in the *Iliad* 6.123-231). Some could even claim a degree of superiority because of 'divine descent' (such as 'Homer's Achilles, Vergil's Aeneas, and Statius' Theseus' [Bernstein 2008: 10]). Furthermore, lines of descent, which were typically androcentric, functioned both as an indicator of attributed status and an index of potential character (Bernstein 2003: 353-55). To be called someone's son or daughter thus was not only an indication of a figure's social identity but an announcement of the qualities by which the son or daughter potentially would be defined. Luke's inclusion of the illustrious genealogy of Jesus (Lk. 3.23-38), for example, is not an innocuous decoration. This is the Third Gospel's emphatic declaration of the superior identity and character of Jesus.

Although Mark's professional biography did not include Jesus' human ancestry, Mark's first scenes (1.1-15) declare the superior identity and character of the one who will shortly be introduced as a disciple-gathering teacher (1.16-20; 2.13-14). With the Markan Jesus hearing a voice that announces 'You are my Son' (1.11), Mark indicates the superiority of Jesus to any of the Gospel's other dramatis personae. Such a declaration is only made to Jesus (cf. 9.7; 12.6; cf. 3.11; 15.39). Furthermore, in Mark's Gospel, Jesus is the only character who will directly say 'Abba' ('Father' in Aramaic; 14.36) or 'Eloi' ('My God' in Aramaic; 15.34) near the close of his ministry. Important figures such as the scribes (professional teachers), Herod Antipas, the so-called king, the Sanhedrin officials, or governor Pilate will go across the narrative stage with high status in tow but the narrative spell is already cast for Mark's auditors to distinguish Jesus from all others. Indeed, early on, Mark will distinguish Jesus from the scribes even before they walk on the narrative stage. Thus, at Jesus' first exorcism, Mark will mention that the people of the synagogue were amazed 'because he taught them as one with authority and not as the scribes' (1.22). Likewise, the members of the synagogue will raise the first question about his identity: 'What is this? A new teaching?—and with authority' (1.27). From beginning to end and from private to public moments, the Markan Jesus' prowess is established even if he deflects honor to God and away from himself (Struthers Malbon 2009: 133). Even to welcome someone in his name then is to welcome the one who sent him (9.37; cf. 12.6). Whatever the self-identity of the historical Jesus, the Gospel of Mark elevates the status of Jesus the teacher and therefore heightens the travesty of the accusation that resulted in the death of the one with the claim of divine descent.

The rhetoric of divine descent, however, does more than simply reveal Jesus' social identity. For characters described with a rhetoric of descent, the rhetoric assigns qualities 'perceived by others to have been conferred by their descent' (Bernstein 2008: 10). Unless problematized, the rhetoric forecasts potential for those with an honorable lineage or stigma and embarrassment for those whose heritage is flawed. In the case of Statius's *Thebaid*, for example, Polynices hesitates to introduce himself fully because he is a descendent of Oedipus. If he introduces himself as a descendent of Oedipus, a kin-killer, others in the *Thebaid* narrative world would expect Polynices to be a future kin-killer as well (as indeed tragically becomes the case). Polynices thus is stigmatized by his descent.

In the case of the Markan Jesus, however, divine descent confers the positive and powerful qualities of the deity who stands mostly in the wings off of the narrative stage. If the allusive or intertextual stock repertoire of Mk 1.1-15 is a 'New Exodus' typology (see Chapter 4) based in part on selective texts from Second Isaiah (Isaiah 40–55, specifically, Isa. 43.16-19; 44.26-27; 51.9-11), as many scholars argue (Horsley 2001: 102; Watts 2000: 129-32), the deity behind Mark's Gospel is an active agent of liberation (whether in a first exodus from the tyranny of Pharaoh and Egypt or a second exodus from the tyranny of the Babylonians). The ministry of the Markan teacher Jesus thus will foster the latest version of an exodus liberative movement. Whatever sordid scenes of shame Mark's story would ultimately reveal as the narrative unfolds, then, Mark has already identified Jesus as an active agent of liberation, not as a victim of Rome's tyranny.

The Markan Teacher and the Rhetoric of Achievements
Second, a writer could deploy the rhetoric of deeds, thus brandishing a figure's record of accomplishments, exploits, acts of clemency or beneficence. Valerius Maximus did so in explaining the rise to prominence of Rome's legendary kings and statesmen despite the humble beginnings of such figures (*Memorable Doings and Sayings*, 3.4). Emperors did so through their *Res gestae* (Latin for 'things done'), which typically—as in the cases of Augustus and Vespasian—identified their piety (e.g. in the restoration of temples), peace (in ending civil wars), powers (mastery over land and sea), and patronage (in the granting of privileges, petitions for positions, and promotions to others; e.g. see *Res gestae divi Augustus* 15-20; cf. Suetonius, *Vespasian*, 8-9). In the case of Vespasian whose rise to power was not expected (because he was not connected by blood or adoption lines to the Julio-Claudian emperors who preceded him), such a record of accomplishments trumpeted loudly his ability to overcome an unremarkable and ordinary past, to rise through the ranks of the *cursus honorum* (the standard course of magistrative offices typically pursued to receive honor and thus bring greater social standing—if not also greater wealth—to one's family [Beacham 1999: 34]), and to become the first of the Flavian emperors. In later Flavian lore, Vespasian was known as a wonder worker, having healed both a blind man and a lame man (Suetonius, *Vespasian*, 7.2-3; cf. Luke 2010).

Mark repeatedly touts Jesus' accomplishments, though the Markan Jesus himself refrains from promoting his own fame. Villagers in Nazareth acknowledge Jesus' wisdom *and* brokerage power, as if they are summarizing the Gospel's narrative since Jesus began to call disciples (6.2; cf. 1.16–6.1). Some outsiders summarize his achievements with the Greek perfect tense (which captures completed action in the past with continuing results): 'He has done all things well' (cf. 7.37).

His accomplishments also include repetitive desert miracles, which reveal Jesus' compassionate brokerage style and reenact utopian scenes of abundance (Pervo 1994: 174, 176) from the repertoire of God's liberative acts in Israel's past (6.31-44; 8.1-10). Furthermore, repetitive accounts of the healing of blind men (8.22-26 and 10.46-52) in the course of a journey from Galilee to Jerusalem reveal Jesus' power to reclaim Isaianic promises even if by now his disciples have departed from the Septuagint brokerage styles that best characterize the tenor of Jesus' service to others.

Thus, these and many other accomplishments elevate the status of Jesus long before the teacher suffers a litany of insults in the closing scenes of this Gospel's lore. His posture of prayer and thanks to the deity signals his piety. His many miracles broker the deity's beneficence to those perceiving a need for the deity's latest brand of exodus liberation. Faced with the sheer explosion of need around him, he even calls and commissions disciples who are authorized to mediate the deity's beneficence through word and deed (3.13-19 and 6.6b-13, 30). Such consonance between speech and action was an ancient philosophical ideal. Indeed, again, 'He has done all things well' (cf. 7.37).

The Markan Teacher and the Rhetoric of Dying Well
Third, a writer could bolster a figure's status by deploying the rhetoric of dying well. Here, the writer would give the figure a good exit, which typically included a calm death, consistency in death as in life, the company of friends, and a proper burial. In those instances in which a famous figure died unjustly, a writer could appeal to 'noble death' typologies to demonstrate a valiant death.

Among the Greeks, for example, some valiant deaths were a part of a Greek genre known as *Teleutai* (or 'Deaths'). These brief collections were frequently told about defiant figures who lived during the reigns of the emperors Tiberius, Nero, and Domitian (Burridge 2004: 74). Focused on a hero's death, such collections also inspired later tales such as the *Acta Alexandrinorum*, a collection of martyrdom accounts about a hero facing a tyrant (Harker 2008: 141).

Among the Romans, the *exitus illustrium virorum*, a subtype of the Greek *Teleutai* genre, offered biographical eulogies of the suffering and deaths of famous men. Some laudatory biographical pamphlets recalled the valiant stances of Cato the Younger against Julius Caesar in the republican era. Thus, they were more than eulogies. They were written to make dissident statements against the princeps (imperial ruler) in the period of the Principate. As David Aune has noted, Cato the Younger 'became an ideological symbol of the virtues of Republican Rome, and became the focus of a propaganda war' (1987: 35-36).

Among the Jews, the valiant deaths of Eleazar, an unnamed woman, and her seven sons were lauded. Eleazar, the aforementioned mother, and her seven sons all embraced the character of a 'martyr' long before the term had ever come into use to describe persons willing to die for their faith. In a story-world set in second-century BCE Maccabean times, these nine proto-martyrs unwaveringly confronted the tyrant Antiochus IV, a Greek Seleucid king. All were 'righteous sufferers', like Joseph in Genesis 37–39; Susanna in chapter 13 of the Greek version of Daniel; or Daniel in Daniel 6 (Nickelsburg 1980: 153-84). All were also brave; all exposed the rage of a brutal king; yet none denied their deity or their convictions to assuage the tyrant's wrath (2 Macc. 6.16–7.42). Tales of their suffering and deaths would later influence the Book of Hebrews, the writings of Ignatius, and the Acts of Christian martyrs (MacMullen 1966: 84, 89). As we shall see, their valiant exits, also were influenced by Socratic ideals.

According to some scholars, the so-called passion narratives of the Gospels are similar to the aforementioned *Teleutai* (Burridge 2004: 74; cf. Yarbro Collins 2007: 627-39). Indeed, Mark includes episodic anecdotes of suffering and death in what may be called the 'passions' of its two principal prophets—John and Jesus—respectively in Mark 6 and 14–15. These 'passions' are thematically structured in similar ways in that a venerated figure suffers and dies because of the ruthless actions of one of Rome's representatives. Thus, a hero is brought before a tyrant before whom the hero—whether John or Jesus—dies an unjust death.

Yet, Mark's 'passions' interest is not limited to Mark 6 and 14–15. As early as Mk 1.14, John is arrested or handed over. Ominous notices about the suffering and death of Jesus are also forecast in 2.19 and 3.6, and again, most notably, in the three passion/resurrection prediction subunits in Mark 8–10. Coverage of the opposition to Jesus along with his suffering and death, moreover, is extended over much of the remaining chapters of the Gospel (Mark 11–15). Thus, while Mark may not be adequately labeled as a passion narrative with a long introduction (to paraphrase Martin Kähler's evaluation of the Gospel [Kähler 1964: 80 n. 11]), it is a Gospel with a strong emphasis on the 'passions' of its principal prophetic emissaries throughout its narrative and it projects that Jesus' own disciples will be subjected to 'passions' as well (13.9-13).

So, how would Mark depict Jesus as dying well? While Chapter 2 (on Jesus as a Prophetic Envoy) and Chapter 5 (on Jesus as a Philosophical Hero) will carefully explain how Mark used well-known typological founts to explain to auditors why Jesus died in such an ignominious and unjust way, a few general remarks about his good exit are critical now.

As a teacher *in life*, as noted in the previous chapter, Jesus modeled how his disciples should live virtuous lives. Such lives needed to be free of greed, guile, and a quest for glory. Yet, Jesus was no less a model teacher *at the doors of death*. In an apocalyptic discourse given shortly before his death (13.3-37), Jesus prepares his learners for the coming days. Having taught *in* the temple (12.13-44) and after *walking out of* the temple (13.1-2), he also teaches *opposite* the temple while sitting on the Mount of Olives (13.3-37). While Jesus' rather extended discourse is sometimes known as the 'little apocalypse' (13.3-37) in opposition to the 'great apocalypse' or Revelation (Marcus 2009: 865; Donahue and Harrington 2002: 378), the discourse also has the tenor of a farewell discourse, with a venerated figure sharing the fate and fortunes of his followers in the shadows of his own departure. In either case, Jesus continues his role as a teacher. That is, he takes on the seated posture of a teacher imparting a farewell message about the tyrannical times that his disciples would soon face for themselves (13.13). Also, his multiple warnings and challenges to watch, not to wander (cf. 13.5, 6, 9, 22, 33), or to stay awake (13.35, 36) all conclude with parables (13.28-37), his characteristic mode of teaching. Furthermore, the first of his farewell parables begins with the imperative 'learn' (*mathete*, 13.28).

If Mark's auditors noted how Mark's Gospel built 'passion' diction, they would have known that much of the purpose of Jesus' teaching in the apocalyptic farewell discourse material was to prepare his disciples for the inevitability of their own 'passions' before authority figures (13.9-13). That is, select diction of Mark's passion/resurrection prediction units prepares the audience to be attuned to a type of 'passion' diction that they would see in 13.9-13.

So, for example, each prediction unit lists the *source* of the suffering, rejection, or abuse that the Son of the Human One (or the 'Son of Man') will face: elders, chief priests, and scribes in the first prediction (8.31); the hands of 'people' in the second prediction (9.31); and chief priests and scribes along with Gentiles in the third prediction (10.33). It should be known, moreover, that the opponents in the first prediction essentially were the constituents of the Sanhedrin (*synedrion*) or Council (cf. 15.1).

Two of the passion/resurrection predictions also use a form of *paradidōmi* (which was first used to describe the 'arrest' of John as early as 1.14) to indicate the *means* by which Jesus will come before the authorities. Thus, in the second prediction unit, Jesus asserts that the Son of Man will be 'handed over' or 'delivered up' (*paradidotai*) into the hands of people' (9.31) while cognates of *paradidōmi* appear twice in the longer, third passion/resurrection prediction unit. Thus, the Son of the Human One 'will be handed over' (*paradothēsetai*) to the chief priests and scribes (10.33) and they, in turn, 'will hand him over' (*paradōsousin*) to the Gentiles (10.33).

All three passion/resurrection prediction units also predict the ultimate *telos* or end of the abuse that Jesus suffers, namely, death. Even if an audience did not clearly understand the specific nature of the suffering that the Son of the Human One would face because of the nebulous diction of 'suffering' (*pathein*) in the first prediction unit, the necessity of resurrection itself infers unambiguously that Jesus would die (8.31). The second prediction unit is unmistakably clear by its repetition of 'kill' words: 'they will *kill* (*apoktenousin*) him, and *after being killed* (*apoktantheis*), he will arise' (9.31). Unmistakable as well is the force of the third prediction unit, which both speaks of a 'condemnation' (*katakrinō*) that will result in death (*thanatos*) and deploys a 'kill' word (*apokteinō*, 10.34).

So, altogether, the three units speak about the agents of suffering, the 'delivery/arrest/betrayal' (*paradidōmi*) mechanism by which the Son of the Human One will face suffering, and the ultimate fate of death (see Diagram 3). In the passion narrative proper, these same three elements are featured. (1) the Sanhedrin or Council seeks to find a way to kill him (14.1, 53; 15.1); (2) Jesus endures a series of 'deliveries' that ultimately bring him to his fate (14.10-11, 18, 21, 41-42, 44; 15.1, 10, 15); and (3) death is the ultimate fate that Jesus endures before God vindicates him through resurrection. While various parts of the Council seek to kill him (14.1), they also seek witnesses in order 'to put him to death' (*eis to thanatōsai*, 14.55). In the end, all 'condemn' (*katakrinō*) him as deserving 'death' (*thanatos*, 14.64).

Diagram 3
*The Sources, Means, and Telos (or End) of Jesus' Suffering
in the Three Passion/Resurrection Prediction Units*

	Unit 1	Unit 2	Unit 3
Source	Elders, Chief priests, Scribes (8.31)	hands of people (9.31)	Chief priests, Scribes, Gentiles (10.33-34)
Means	x	delivery/betrayal *paradidōmi* diction (9.31)	delivery betrayal *paradidōmi* diction (10.33 [twice])
Telos	death with kill diction (8.31)	death with kill diction 9.31)	death with kill and condemnation to death diction (10.33-34)

Mark 13.9-13 certainly has the aforementioned 'passion' diction. The future difficulties of Jesus' followers include at the least the agents or *sources* (councils, governors, and kings, 13.9) of the disciples' suffering. Also, to indicate the *means* by which the disciples will face future suffering, the Markan Jesus will repeat the *paradidōmi* (arrest/deliver up/betray) diction three times (13.9, 11-12). Furthermore, the ultimate negative *telos* or fate for these believers is death. As Jesus predicts. 'brother will deliver

up brother to *death* (*thanatos*) and father…child; and children will rise up against parents and *kill* them (*thanatoō*, 13.12). Thus, Mk 13.9-13 appears to be the prediction of the 'passion' of Jesus' followers in the future (see Diagram 4).

Diagram 4
The 'Passion' of 13.9-13

Source	Councils, Governors, Kings	13.9
Means	delivery/betrayal (*paradidōmi*) diction	13.9, 11-12
Telos	death with condemnation to death diction	13.12

That Jesus exited well is made all the more clear through Mark's inter-lacement or narrative volley of episodes back-and-forth about Jesus and Peter as they faced authority figures. In 14.53, Jesus is led away (*apagō*) by the arresting party to the high priest. In 14.54, Peter follows at a distance. In 14.55-65, Jesus appears before the high priest and the whole Council (*synedrion*), to whom he answers nothing except to say 'I am' (*egō eimi*) when asked whether he was 'Christ, the Son of the Blessed One' and to announce the status (the legitimate right to sit at the right hand of power) and coming of the Son of the Human One (14.61-62). Then, in 14.66-72, the narrative returns yet again to Peter who denies being with the Nazarene, Jesus, or even knowing him.

As many commentators have noticed, the back-and-forth movement of the scenes gives the appearance that the two events are occurring simulta-neously (Rhoads, Dewey and Michie 1999: 51). At the least, the suspen-sion of story lines about Peter and the resumption of such story lines to tell where Peter was located (in the courtyard, 14.53, 66) and what he was doing (warming himself) suggest that Peter's response to his interlocu-tors is temporally close to the time of Jesus' response to his interlocutors. Even Peter's movement out from (*exō*) the courtyard (*aulē*) to the fore-court (*proaulion*, 14.68) contributes to this resumptive impulse. That is, it reminds auditors that Peter earlier had followed Jesus into (*esō*) the court-yard (14.53). Heightening the sense of comparison is the contrast between the narrative's use of forms of the verb 'to be' (*eimi*) to describe Jesus' lone response and the use of the verb *eimi* in the descriptions of Peter given by his interlocutors. So, on the one hand, Jesus declares *egō eimi* ('I am', 14.62). On the other hand, with the *eimi* form *estin* ('is'), the high priest's servant declares about Peter: 'This one is (*estin*) of them' (14.69). Simi-larly, more interrogators later use the *eimi* form *ei* ('are') to identify Peter as an associate with Jesus. 'Truly, you are (*ei*) one of them, for you are (*ei*) a Galilean' (14.70).

What would not go unnoticed by auditors with ears to hear, moreover, are the connections between the interlacement in 14.53-72 and earlier portions of the Gospel. First, an obvious connection is Jesus' prediction of Peter's denial (14.27-31). That connection builds irony (a disparity between the knowledge of select characters on the one hand and the knowledge of the auditors on the other) because one of Jesus' predictions actually comes to pass shortly after his mockers ask him to prophesy (14.65).

Second, the initial description of Peter given by the high priest's servant is a familiar refrain throughout the Gospel. That is, Jesus calls the disciples to be 'with him' (*met' autou*, 3.14). The Gerasene man, from whom the demons were cast out, wants to go 'with' Jesus (*met' autou*, 5.18). In the crucible, though, the solidarity that Jesus seeks to build seems to fall apart. While Jesus seeks to be 'with' (*meta*) his disciples (14.14, 17), the narrative depicts the arrival of Judas (one of the twelve) and the arresting party that comes 'with him' (*met' autou*, 14.43)—that is, with Judas. In that context, then, the high priest's servant poignantly says to Peter. 'You were *with* (*meta*) the Nazarene' (14.67).

Third, as seen in Diagram 5, auditors with ears to hear would likely connect the interlacement in 14.53-72 with Jesus' prediction that his disciples would face scenes of interrogation (13.9-13). Jesus predicted that his disciples would be handed over (*paradidōmi*, 13.9) and hustled up (literally 'led [away]', *agō*, 13.11), both of which happen to him in the Gospel's closing scenes (cf. 14.44 and 14.53, respectively). He also mentioned the *synedria* (or the Councils, 13.9) as one set of authority figures before whom the disciples might be handed over. Jesus himself faced the *synedrion* in the heat of the crucible (14.55). Furthermore, he predicted the possibility of interrogation or—at the least—scenes in which the disciples would have to give an answer presumably to accusations raised by the authorities to whom they are handed over. The whole of the interlacement in 14.53-72 entails interrogation.

Diagram 5
Links between 13.9-13 and 14.53-72

	13.9-13	14.53-72
Led Away Diction	*agō* (13.11)	*apagō* (14.53)
Synedria Diction	councils (13.12)	Council (14.55) witnesses
Witness Diction	witness/testimony (13.9)	witnesses (14.55-56, 59-60; cf. 14.63)
Death Diction	*thanatos, thanatoō* (13.12)	*eis to thanatōsai, thanatos* (14.55, 64)

Thus, Mark's interlacement in 14.53-72, if it is a comparison between Jesus and Peter at some level, reveals how disciples should respond in the face of Rome's brokering authorities (whether those are brokers from local provinces or ones appointed directly by Rome). Mark suggests that Jesus' followers who are the deity's own brokers in the world should not respond as Peter did. Indeed, Mark positions Peter's response in the flow of multiple incorrect responses to the possibility of being handed over. Accordingly, auditors should not respond as the twelve and another unnamed disciple responded at Jesus' arrest, namely, with flight before the possibility of interrogation (14.50-52). Nor should they respond as did Peter who denied his association with Jesus under interrogation. Instead, the correct response is given by Jesus who confirms his true identity. Apparently, as predicted by Jesus, the Holy Spirit would give his followers what they needed to say should they face their own 'passions' (13.11).

If the connections between Mk 13.9-13 and Mk 14.53-72 are convincing, Mark has strategically integrated these parts such that Jesus the teacher 'on trial' becomes a model for disciples in their future 'trials', a point noticed long ago in Donahue's study, *'Are You the Christ?': The Trial Narrative in the Gospel of Mark* (1973). That is, the interlacement of the 'trial' of Jesus with the 'trial' of Peter is not isolated from the rest of the story any more than any part of the so-called passion account is isolated. Indeed, the 'passion' narrative bears an intertextual, compositional, and thematic consistency with everything that precedes it (Kelber 1976: 153-80). If Mark's auditors faced persecution or feared its threat in a context when they were being handed over (13.9, 11-12) to Rome's authorities, Mark's story about Jesus puts Jesus and Peter in a context where both are interrogated, where one has been handed over, and the other faces a similar fate when he is identified as being 'with' Jesus. Jesus alone, though, models the endurance his followers will need to emulate. He exits well.

Summary

Faced with the challenge of recasting the shame associated with Jesus' ignominious death, then, Mark's story about Jesus reshaped the memory of Jesus the teacher and his movement away from the perception of failure. While Christianity likely faced criticism because of Jesus' shameful death, Mark insisted that Jesus was not a charlatan characterized by greed, guile, or a quest for glory. Mark deployed the 'rhetoric of descent' to reveal Jesus' superior social identity and potential character. Mark also deployed a 'rhetoric of achievement' that trumpeted the teacher's virtuous words and deeds. Finally, Mark deployed a rhetoric of dying well to depict Jesus' death as a valiant exit in which Jesus prepared his followers for their future 'passions'. Mark's biography then is a *Life* about a teacher. Still, it is more than just a tale about a teacher. Mark's Gospel presents a wide narrative scope, one in which Jesus spends time with a variety of followers. In doing so, Jesus the teacher calls, commissions, and corrects many of his followers to prepare them to be virtuous followers. While the inclusion of so much information about Jesus' followers may well be a rhetorical device that puts Jesus' teaching content on display, that information also informs Mark's earliest auditors on how best to follow Jesus (or how not to follow him) and thus avoid apostasy. As we shall see in the subsequent chapter, then, Mark is more than a story about a teacher. It is also an inspirational story for the teacher's learners or followers, especially those who would have been the earliest auditors of Mark's *Life*.

Chapter 2

MARK AS A *LIFE* FOR JESUS' FOLLOWERS

Introduction

In what is often considered to be the most historically transparent part of
Mark's Gospel (13.9-13), Jesus warns his disciples that they will 'stand
before governors and kings' (13.9; cf. Donahue 1973: 212-24; Tannehill
1980: 142). In the narrative itself, both John and Jesus meet their fate as
they appear respectively before (one who is called) a 'king' (6.14-29) and
a governor (15.1-15). Both are brutally put to death because of their consistent prophetic messages even in the face of tyrannical pressures. Thus,
both Jesus' warning to his disciples and his charge that they endure (13.13)
arguably mean that the disciples are also urged to take on prophetic stances
in pressure-filled times. Yet, the Gospel's closing scenes would suggest that
the disciples in the narrative fail miserably in that effort. Instead of exhibiting endurance or signs of allegiance to their convictions in the face of
struggles, the disciples in the narrative only show failure as demonstrated
in betrayal, flight, denial, and fear. Listening in on the narrative, though,
are Mark's auditors—disciples located outside of the narrative. Apparently,
Jesus' warning and charge also invite the earliest auditors of the Gospel
to become faithful messengers (to take on prophetic stances of endurance)
despite the shame-laden pressures of their own times.

So, although the Gospel of Mark is a story *about* Jesus, it is also a story
for others, for audiences that may have been hustled up before authorities on
trumped-up charges. This chapter will argue that the key rhetorical goal of
the Gospel is to provide inspiration for those auditors who were experiencing the travails listed in the 'hardship list' (the peristasis catalogue) of 13.9-
13. As the previous chapter noted, a key reason for the contrast between
Jesus and Peter in the interlacement of scenes in Mk 14.53-72 was to depict
Jesus as the best model for Markan auditors who faced or feared the threats
predicted by Jesus in Mk 13.9-13. That the Gospel prepares auditors to
endure the shame-ridden travails of Jesus' prediction (13.13) is revealed
in at least three others ways: (1) in the discipleship orientation by which
Mark's earliest auditors conceivably would have heard the whole Gospel's
acoustical arrangement; (2) in the Gospel's contrast between models of

courage (the so-called 'little people' [Black 2001: 233) and models of cowardice (some of Jesus' disciples); and (3) in the Gospel's prediction of discipleship rehabilitation off of the narrative stage.

The Discipleship Orientation of Mark's Whole Story

The scrolls on which the Gospel of Mark first appeared did not include first-
century back-flap blurbs to provide a commentary on Mark's Gospel. Thus,
we cannot know exactly how Mark's earliest auditors would have heard
oral performances of Mark's story of rejection. Yet, the Gospel does seem
to have coherence. As a biographical work that deploys a popular style, the
Gospel of Mark is a fairly continuous narrative that deploys both chronological and topical structure in its development. Thus, on the one hand, the
Gospel charts Jesus' adult teaching ministry chronologically from his baptism to his passion and resurrection. In doing so, it also interweaves a brief
'life' of John. John's adult ministry in the wilderness (1.4-13); his arrest
(1.14); and ultimately his death by beheading (6.17-29; cf. 9.13). On the
other hand, the Gospel fills in 'the exterior framework of a chronological
sequence with topical material' (Burridge 2004: 196). Mark structures the
'topical material', which is largely based on the interrelated typologies of a
prophetic envoy, a powerful broker, and a philosophical hero, across a narrative that may be construed as three basic units. (1) the sending forth of
two principal prophetic emissaries/brokers, John and Jesus (1.1-15); (2) the
teaching or preparation of others who will be sent out (or who will go out)
as prophetic emissaries/brokers (1.16-10.52); and (3) the final crucible or
most intense moments of suffering for a heroic emissary and broker (11.1–
16.8). Thus, all three units presuppose the deity's authorization of emissar-
ies/brokers, with Jesus both being sent by the deity and yet sending others
on behalf of the deity.

As Mark's earliest auditors heard the story of the deity's authorization
of prophetic emissaries, they could assess their own suffering and possible deaths in the light of this larger story. They could also look to John and
Jesus as adequate prophetic paradigms on how they themselves could resist
Rome's imperial powers. On the one hand, the resistance could be viscer-
ally physical, as both John and Jesus physically faced the ruthlessness of
tyrannical pressures. On the other hand, the resistance could be internal, as
both John and Jesus clashed with the values of the Roman imperial order.

Accordingly, the first unit (1.1-15), which is organized exclusively on
the basis of the emergence of John and Jesus, depicts their confirmation as
prophetic emissaries/brokers who have been sent out by the deity to others.
They appear as autonomous emissaries/ brokers, without connections to the
established centers of authority. They are confirmed by their reenactments
of a prophetic script. That is, they fit the profile of Septuagint prophetic

emissaries/brokers, especially on the order of an Elijah-like messenger type. Despite the confirmation of these two principal prophets, the Gospel sounds early on an ominous note about how these prophets will be received (1.14).

While the second unit (1.16–10.52) includes multiple episodes with three stages (see Diagram 6 below), it appears to be organized around Jesus' efforts to prepare others to be prophetic emissaries/brokers. Formal *call* episodes (1.16-20; 2.13-14) organize two other blocks of episodes about the growth of Jesus' prophetic fame and the growth of the opposition to his work (1.21–2.12; 2.15–3.6). Formal *commissioning* scenes (3.13-19 [with a prefatory summary, 3.7-12] and 6.6b-13 [with a narrative transition and flashback on John's 'passion', 6.14-29], 30) frame a pattern of episodes (3.19b–6.6a) that show ever growing signs of prophetic rejection toward Jesus' word, work, and identity as an authorized prophetic envoy. The framed material itself (4.1–5.43) forms an a-b-b'-a' chiastic pattern (see Diagram 6 below) that highlights the growing mis-recognition of Jesus' true identity, even as it emphasizes how certain ostensible insiders and intimate character groups (those who should be closest to Jesus) are becoming like outsiders. Then, in what may be called a 'bread' section (with two feeding episodes, 6.31-44; 8.1-9) and a 'blindness' section (with the healings of two blind men, 8.22-26 and 10.46-52), Mark depicts Jesus seeking to *correct* the disciples, that is, to help them hear, see, or understand his Septuagint-based brokerage style.

Accordingly, in the bread section (6.31–8.21), Mark's two feeding episodes with their 'boat-trip conclusions' (6.31-52 and 8.1-21) frame yet other episodes (6.53–7.37) in which outsiders are more adept in participating in the restorative work of the rule of God than are insiders (Tolbert 1996: 178). In the blindness section (8.22–10.52), moreover, Mark's two accounts of the healing of a blind man (8.22-26 and 10.46-52) frame yet other episodes (8.27–10.45) in which the blindness of Jesus' own disciples is exposed and explained as Jesus seeks to lead his followers on the New Exodus way. Altogether, in this second unit, auditors learn how Jesus and such disciples appear to be moving in different directions. That is, while Jesus appears to follow the brokerage style of prophetic scripts from Israel's heritage, his disciples' brokering style seems more in alignment with select, established types of brokerage that the Gospel seeks to contest. So, although twelve of his disciples were called to be his intimates, to be with him (3.14), their interest in fame and rank make them appear more like the Pharisees and the Herodians that Mark stylizes as unjust or inept brokers throughout the Gospel. Thus, a clash of brokerage styles lies at the heart of Mark's story.

The third unit (11.1–16.8) concludes Mark's story by depicting the most intense moments of conflict that Jesus and his band of prophetic brokers will face in the Gospel. More specifically, the unit covers the arrival of Jesus and his band of followers into Jerusalem, clashes between the brokering styles of Jesus and that of the Jerusalem authorities, and an inspirational portrait of Jesus' fidelity as a heroic model for those who will face tyrannical pressures in their own times. Mark fully shifts the setting of Jesus' ministry from Galilee to Jerusalem, where Jesus demonstrates his knowledge of scripture and of the future and he provides, as Mary Ann Tolbert has suggested, 'an example of faithful, watchful endurance through suffering, persecution, and even death' (1996: 275). At the same time, 11.1–16.8 is a study of contrasts. With an overall presentation of 'mounting opposition', a fracturing fellowship, and recognition (or misrecognition), the closing scenes of the Gospel present the climactic testing moments for Jesus and his disciples (Donahue 1982: 570). Thus, these scenes show the drastic difference between the readiness of Jesus and the un-readiness of the disciples for the growing opposition. During these final testing periods, Jesus— as example—is watchful and ready; the disciples are not. Because of his knowledge, Jesus is able to endure the crucible before Jewish and Roman authorities, the very request he made to his disciples in the Olivet apocalyptic/farewell discourse (13.9-13).

Diagram 6

The Rhetorical Structure of Mark's Second Unit

Stage One: The Call of Disciples as Brokers (1.16–3.6)
A   Call of Four Disciples: 1.16-20
B   A Series of Miracle Episodes: 1.21–2.12
A' Call of One Disciple: 2.13-14
B' A Series of Controversy Episodes: 2.15–3.6

Stage Two: The Commissioning of Disciples as Brokers (3.7–6.30)
First Commission (3.13-19; with a prefatory summary, 3.7-12)
A   Misrecognition of a Prophet's Source of Power (3.20-35)
B   Hearing the Truth about the Restorative Rule of God (4.1-34)
B' Enacting God's Restoration (4.35–5.43)
A' Misrecognition of a Prophet's Source of Power (6.1–6.6a)
Second Commission (6.6b-13, 30, with a narrative transition and flashback, 6.14-29)

Stage Three: Correcting the Disciples as Brokers (6.31–10.52)
Feeding the 5000 and the Boat Trip Conclusion (6.31-52)
A   Requests for Restoration or Release (6.53-56)
B   Insiders' Responses to a Food Riddle (7.1-23)
B' An Outsider's Responses to a Food Riddle (7.24-30)
A' Requests for Restoration or Release (7.31-37)
Feeding the 4000 and the Boat Trip Conclusion (8.1-21)
A   Healing of a Blind Man (8.22-26)
B   The Identity of Jesus (8.27-30) and Three Passion/Resurrection Prediction Patterns (8.31–10.45)
A' Healing of Blind Bartimaeus (10.46-52)

Mark's Contrasting Models of Courage and Cowardice

A perennial problem in Markan scholarship has been determining why the Gospel has such a negative view of the disciples. Relatedly, Markan scholars have also wondered what is the function of the positive portrait of the so-called 'little people', those who make cameo appearances on the narrative stage. If Mark's story is not solely *about* Jesus as a teacher but also *for* his followers, perhaps the two contrasting portraits (on the order of the contrast between Jesus and Peter in the interlacement of 14.53-72) aid the Markan auditors in knowing both how to face difficult times and how not to face difficult times. They learn what produces courage and what does not.

The Function of the Markan Suppliants Character Group
Mark includes several similarly constructed suppliant episodes, that is, episodes where suppliants seek help for themselves or for others, namely, the episodes that feature the faithful four who brought the paralytic to Jesus (2.1-12), the 'woman in the crowd' (as she is named by Mary Ann Tolbert [1992: 354], 5.24b-35), the Syrophoenician woman (7.24-30), and Bartimaeus (Mk 10.46-52). The suppliants in these episodes are sometimes called the 'little people' because they (among others) only make a cameo appearance on the narrative stage (Black 2001: 233). In such an appearance, though, the suppliants are similar in at least four ways. First, the 'little people' are mostly anonymous. We do not know the names of the four men who brought their friend to Jesus in 2.1-12. The identity of the woman in the crowd in Mark 5 remains unknown. The woman whose daughter needs healing in 7.24-30 is described as a Greek and as a Syrophoenician but her name does not receive notice. Even the actual name of the blind man in Mk 10.46-52 remains hidden. We simply know that he is the son of Timaeus.

Second, all of the 'little people' seek help again for themselves or for others because they live in a society that looks contemptuously on persons whose bodies departed from a so-called physical ideal. In the so-called Ancient Near East cultures and in Greek and Roman cultures of the New Testament period, bodily differences mattered because so-called de-graded bodies departed from ideological physical ideals of wholeness. In certain biblical texts such as Lev. 21.16-23, for example, blindness, lameness, or a broken hand rendered a person unable to participate in a ritual sacrifice (Barasch 2001: 15). Likewise, in Greek and Roman cultures, a physical ideal of beauty is presupposed as a norm against which all other bodily forms were measured. Thus, in answer to the question—'How to recognize a newborn child that is worth raising?'—second-century CE Soranus responds that the child 'should be perfect in all its parts, limbs and senses, and have passages that are not obstructed, including ears, nose, throat, urethra and anus. Its natural movements should be neither slow nor feeble, its limbs should bend and stretch, its size and shape should be appropriate, and it should respond to external stimuli' (*Gynaecology*, 2.6.5). So, the suppliants coming to Jesus seek out his restorative power as promised, for example, in Isa. 35.6.

Third, all of these suppliants are motivated to go to Jesus by what they have heard about Jesus. So, in 2.1-12, 'it was *noised* (*akouō*) that he [Jesus] was at home' Literally, 'it was *heard* that he was at home' (2.1). In 5.24b-35, 'she [the woman in the crowd] *had heard* (*akouō*) about Jesus' (5.27). In 7.24-30, 'but a woman whose daughter had an unclean spirit immediately *heard* (*akouō*) about him' (7.25). In 10.46-52, 'when he [Bartimaeus] *heard* (*akouō*) that it was Jesus of Nazareth' (10.47), he cried out for help.

Fourth, from all appearances, all of these 'little people' have faith or—based on the evidence before us—they have the ability to take agency and thus overcome an obstacle with a relentless resolve. So, when faced with the obstacle of a hindering crowd, the four who brought their friend are willing to un-thatch a roof to present the paralytic before Jesus (2.1-12). Amazingly, the auditors are told that Jesus saw their faith (2.5). Thus, faith in Mark is not so much a cognitive belief as much as it is something people demonstrate. Whatever the struggle of the woman that Mark describes as having a *mastix* ('affliction', lit. 'whip', 5.34), her beating had not recently begun. Rather, the whipping's hostile take-over had now entered its twelfth year. In a remarkable burst of seven participles nowhere else present in the Gospel, Mark summarizes the woman's difficulties and yet notes her agency and relentlessness. To paraphrase Mark's description of the woman:

And a woman
  (1) being with a flow of blood for twelve years
  (2) and having suffered many things from many doctors
  (3) and having spent all the things belonging to her
  (4) and not having benefitted but
  (5) having become worse
  (6) having heard about Jesus
  (7) having gone in the crowd behind [him] touched his garment (5.25-27).

Despite her efforts, she could not relieve herself of the *mastix* nor could the money that she depleted on medical savants bring her to a better state. Instead, she was left worse. Yet, now facing the obstacle of a crowd and perhaps legal regulatory restrictions, she made her way to Jesus. Thus, Jesus commends her for her faith, that is, for her persistence.

While the word 'faith' is not used to describe the Syrophoenician woman (7.24-30), she is clearly relentless. Jesus seeks privacy (7.24b), which she crashes (7.25). Jesus assaults her with classical invective diction that could be hurled against an outsider (about which more must be said later), but the woman throws his 'little dog' insult back on him (7.27-28). So, if faith is relentless resolve, she has passed the test twice over. Likewise, the blind son of Timaeus is relentless. Facing the obstacle of a crowd that would prefer blind people to be silent if not also unseen and just a part of a given scene's ambience, 'he continued to cry out' (*krazō*, 10.48), as is evident by Mark's use of the Greek imperfect. Jesus also commends him for his faith (10.52).

Yet, how are these suppliants related to the 'hardship list' (peristasis catalogue) of 13.9-13? In the face of their own pressures, these suppliants are relentless. They thus establish a pattern for Mark's auditors who face rejection of one sort or another. These so-called 'little people' set the tone for the fidelity that Jesus will model for disciples and request of his disciples in crucible or pressure-filled times. Thus, if faith or persistence truly saved (*sōzō*) both the woman in the crowd (5.34) and Bartimaeus (10.52), disciples will be saved (*sōzō*) in the face of their own pressures by nothing less than faith or persistence/endurance (13.13). These suppliants' relentlessness then marks them as models of courage.

The Function of the Markan Disciples Character Group
If the suppliants are presented in a positive light, the same cannot be said about most of Jesus' disciples. They appear to be just the opposite of the suppliants. Initially, Mark's earliest auditors could have had favorable impressions of the disciples. Mark's emblematic scenes of the calls of the first disciples (1.16-20; 2.13-14) virtually reveal the halcyon days before the opposition's hostility escalates enough to expose the 'implacable' hardness of their hearts (3.1-6, esp. 3.5; Bryan 1993: 90). Initially—like the 'rocky' soil type in the parable of the Sower—the disciple representatives are 'receptive' (4.16). Descriptions of their calls closely follow the Septuagint grid of the call of Elisha (1 Kgs 19.19-21), even if the disciples also look like the student-companions whose summons by an itinerant sage filled the chreiae of ancient biographies (Dowd 2000: 16-18; cf. Yarbro Collins 2007: 156-60). Also, as Jesus' traveling companions (1.21, 29; 2.23), the first called disciples embrace his brokering style. As Sabbath-day suppliants, they actively participate in his restorative brokerage activity on behalf of Simon's mother-in-law (1.29-31) and they register no objections to the extension of the deity's beneficence to those who gather at the door of the house of Simon and Andrew later that evening (1.32-34). They seem eager for all to meet him (1.35-38); and, in the next scene that involves a crowded door, they raise no objections to the destruction of the roof of a house by four other suppliants on behalf of the paralytic (2.1-12). Furthermore, they also embrace his radical inclusivity, that is, his willingness to eat with sinners and toll-collectors (2.16), those who are socially ostracized by polite society.

As the parable of the Sower also suggests, though, 'rocky ground' type characters are capable of falling away under pressure (4.17). In what some scholars would call the 'Stilling of the Storm' pericope (4.35-41), for example, Mark reveals how the disciples lost their stance in faith and took on the role of cowards (*deilos*, 4.40), a term often associated with those who took flight in the face of pressures rather than remaining or enduring when facing them (Josephus, *Jewish Antiquities* 4.298; cf. Herodotus, *Histories* 7.104.5). Unlike the mostly anonymous 'little people', then, Jesus' disciples seemed to have had a problem with obstacles. A sea brings on panic (4.35-41); a relentless spirit residing in a man's son brings on failure (9.14-29); and Jerusalem (the fear of death and perhaps of association with a marginal movement) brings on flight—literally the flight of cowards who despite their earlier insistence of fidelity (14.31) flee from Jesus in the face of the shame-ridden circumstance of Jesus' arrest (14.50).

Why do they fail to act with courage (i.e. consistency or endurance)? Why do they take flight and thus not provide a good model for those who face shame-ridden circumstances among Mark's earliest auditors (again, see 13.9-13)? Mark's bread and blindness sections appear to provide the answers.

In part, both the bread and the blindness sections treat the matter of perception, that is, seeing, hearing, and understanding. Adequate perception (acting on what one has heard), prepares one to be ready to face difficulty. While all of the 'little people' act on what they have heard and thus do not doubt what the broker Jesus is able to do, the disciples, having already witnessed one bread miracle in a desert (6.31-44) wonder if Jesus has the 'power' (or 'is able', *dynamai*) to feed people in another desert (8.1-9, esp. 8.4). The episode about the Syrophoenician woman and her daughter, moreover, confirms that Jesus' brokerage power can even extend to those places to which Jesus has not traveled (7.24-30). Thus, a woman drawn as an outsider seems to have more insight than disciples who were first drawn as insiders. So, although Jesus, while quoting from Isa. 6.9, distinguished outsiders from insiders by describing the former as those who could hear (*akouō*) and yet do not understand (*syniēmi*), it appears that some of his disciples are also without understanding (*asynetos*, 7.18; 8.17; cf. 6.52).

In the blindness section, Jesus not only encounters blind men whom he heals (8.22-26; 10.46-52), but his own disciples seem to lack adequate perception as they seem concerned for rank, fame, and nepotistic ends. Mark carefully arranges this material to show that no matter how much Jesus predicts his suffering, the disciples do not understand him. How many times does he have to tell them before they will no longer see the in-breaking of God's favor in old, outmoded ways? Are they also blind (from the perspective of the sensory metaphors that would have been understood in Mark's day)? The answer is yes, but unfortunately, Jesus does a better job of opening the eyes of those who are physically blind than he does of opening the eyes of his disciples. Unfortunately, he does a better job of healing the eyes of those whom he has only recently met than he does of healing those who have been with him for some time.

In part, the blindness section also reveals another problem for the disciples, their inadequate desire (or will). As several scholars have noted, a critical theme for the Gospel is the matter of having an adequate will, wish, or desire (based on the Greek word *thelō*, 'I want'). Early in the story, Jesus redefines his family as those who do the *will* (*thelēma*) of God (3.35). At the end of his ministry, Jesus prays 'not what I *want* (*thelō*) but what you [want]' (14.36). Diction about the will is also found abundantly in the three passion/resurrection prediction units of Mark 8–10. In the first passion/resurrection prediction unit (8.27–9.29), the *wish* (*thelō*) to follow Jesus (8.34) paradoxically entails the *desire* (*thelō*) to lose life rather than save it (8.35). In the second passion/resurrection prediction unit (9.30–10.31), in a response to the disciples' hidden discussion about the *greatest* (*meizōn*) among them (9.34), Jesus retorts likewise with radical reversal diction: 'if anyone *wants* (*thelō*) to become *first* (*prōtos*), that one must become last and servant of all' (9.35). In the third passion prediction (10.32-52), as a response to James and John's *wish* (*thelō*, 10.35, 10.36) to sit on the right hand and left hand of Jesus in his glory, Jesus retorts yet again with paradoxical force. 'whoever *wants* (*thelō*) to be the *great* (*megas*) among you is to be your servant; and whoever *wants* (*thelō*) to be *first* (*prōtos*) is to be slave of all' (9.43).

In the last passion/resurrection prediction unit, the issue of a proper regard for the 'will' is intensified through a contrast between the 'will' of James and John and that of the suppliant Bartimaeus (10.46-52). To the question, 'What do you (plural) *want* me to do for you?' (*ti thelete [me] poiesō humin*), James and John respond with a request for seats of honor (10.35-36). To the similar question, 'What do you (singular) *want* that I might do for you?' (*ti soi theleis poiēsō*), Bartimaeus asks for the return of his sight (10.51). So, what is Mark suggesting with this surplus of *will* diction? At the least, the *thelō* ('I will, I wish, I want') forms indicate Jesus' attempt to transform the values of his disciples about their own individual lives in preparation for the crucible, that is, the experiences they will have in Jerusalem. Unless they align themselves to the 'will of God' (*thelēma tou theou*, 3.34), as is proper for those belonging to Jesus' new fictive kinship structure, they will not be prepared for the crucible. Ultimately, they were not; only Jesus was, as indicated by his statement: 'Not what I want (*thelō*) but what you [want]' (14.36). Having an adequate desire or a proper regard for the will, then, will be critical for those who will face the shame-ridden circumstances predicted in 13.9-13. In that day as well, Jesus' followers can expect to be separated from their families. When they are handed over by members of their own families—cut off from networks that normally would provide a source of honor—they must do as Jesus did. They must align themselves to the will of God.

The Gospel's Projection of Discipleship Rehabilitation

A Gospel that began with so much promise, with the announcement of the beginning of good news, with the gathering of eager, energetic, and effervescent disciples (1.16-20; 2.13-14) *almost* ends tragically with a crucified Jesus, an empty tomb, and silent male and female disciples. All have taken flight, reinforcing the cowardice that characterized some of Jesus' traveling companions long before Jesus and a band of Galileans made their way into the Judean capital city of Jerusalem. Although 'all' of the disciples said they would not desert Jesus (14.31), all, in fact, deserted him and fled (14.50). Their flight (*pheugō*) is punctuated by the flight (*pheugō*) of the unnamed young follower, a young man who would rather deal with the shame of public nakedness than to be caught continuing to follow Jesus, once the arresting party had arrived (14.51-52). As multiple scholars have noted, just as the first four disciples turned away (*aphiēmi*) from nets and family to follow Jesus (1.16-20) at the *beginning* of the story, disciples now turn away (*aphiēmi*) from Jesus tragically at the *end* of the story (14.50). Furthermore, although two or sometimes three named women disciples witness (*theōreō*, 15.40) the death of Jesus from a distance (15.40-42) or they witness (*theōreō*, 15.47) his burial site (15.40-47), or they witness (*theōreō*, 16.4) the empty tomb, the women at the tomb also moved away in flight (*pheugō*, 16.8).

This story, however, does not end tragically because the Gospel offers signs of reclamation and renewal. In 14.28, Jesus had promised that after the crucible he would go before the disciples in Galilee. And, in 16.7 just before the Gospel ends—in the best of manuscripts—in 16.8, a young man at the tomb reminds women who had gathered there of the place where the reclamation and renewal would take place. He says: 'Go tell his [other] disciples and Peter that he is going ahead of you to Galilee; there you will see him, just as he told you'.

The return to Galilee is a return to a visible landmark, where Jesus had first called and commissioned the disciples. It is the return to a place where the disciples' vision was grounded in the truth that they were conduits of the graces of the deity, not creators of them. They were grounded in the truth that they were sent ones and not the sender.

Of course, 'Go tell his disciples and Peter' is a strange expression. After all, was not Peter a disciple too? Yes, but perhaps the personalizing here is typological. It is for those who, like Peter, failed initially when they faced the shame-ridden circumstances of 13.9-13, for those who themselves had made the great denial ('I am not') while Jesus had made the great confession ('I am'), for those who had also wept bitterly because of their failings, for those who needed a special personalized reminder of the promise of reclamation even for them. The Gospel almost ends tragically but it seems to show a landmark around which Mark's earliest auditors might gather to begin afresh and anew.

Both Jesus' promise to lead his disciples and the promise that they would see him are what make the call to reclamation remarkable. For all the failures, the fickle loyalties, and the fracturing of the fellowship by his disciples, Jesus still promises to lead them, to be their teacher. If perception was a critical problem for the disciples, the Gospel's ending promise is that Jesus' disciples—male and female—would see him. There, the young man at the tomb promises, 'you will see him' (16.7).

Summary

Mark's Gospel is not only a story *about* Jesus. It is a story written *for* the benefit of others, especially those fearing or facing difficult, shame-ridden circumstances in their own times. Mark prepares its earliest auditors for such times primarily through its presentation of a paradigmatic teacher, especially in the Gospel's closing scenes. Yet, the Gospel also prepares its auditors for those times through the acoustical arrangement of the Gospel's complete story. In addition, the Gospel's multiple comparisons and contrasts between the so-called little people on the one hand and some of the disciples on the other hand suggest what is needed in crucible times. Moved by attempts to deal adequately with needful circumstances as opposed to quests for the avoidance of shame or the enhancement of prestige, the little people exhibit courage and relentlessness. By contrast, some of Jesus' disciples seem to lack both the *adequate perception* and the *adequate will or desire* that will prove useful in a crucible. Yet, what if some disciples failed? Is the Gospel only intended to encourage disciples not to go into apostasy? Mark's Gospel seems written for a broader audience. While it is written to help its auditors avoid failure, it also offers hope for those who—like Peter—still need to hear Jesus offering a chance for them to be Jesus' students again and for Jesus to be their teacher again.

Chapter 3

JESUS AS A PROPHETIC ENVOY

Introduction

This chapter argues that Mark deploys the typology of a prophetic envoy to rehabilitate the image of Jesus who may have been perceived as a failed teacher. Initially, the chapter will illustrate Mark's raw exposure of scenes of shame. Mark does not sanitize the scenes as if to deny them altogether. Rather, Mark reveals the brutality of Pilate and his henchmen who were responsible for the laceration of Jesus' flesh and the crucifixion of his body in an extended litany of mockery. Second, in alignment with a *rhetoric of dying well* or a *good exit*, Mark depicts Jesus as a prophetic envoy, as one whose role as a prophet should have brought him the honor due to the deity who had sent him out as a prophetic emissary. Mark also avers that the murder of this prophetic emissary—one of many sent out by the deity—marks a turning point, as indicated in the parable of the Tenants (or the parable of the Dishonored Emissaries). Presenting Jesus then as a prophetic envoy likely bolstered Jesus' image for Mark's earliest auditors. It likely showed that the teacher's death was tragic. It was not a result of failure, but an affront to the God who had sent him forth as a prophet. With such a distinctive apologetic appeal, Mark tried to make sense of Jesus' death.

Showing Raw Scenes of Shame

In the eyes of the ancient Mediterranean, arrest, detention, judicial trial, or final punishment customarily connoted shame. Simply being arrested or being taken into custody could connote shame (cf. 1 Esd. 8.74). Detention, whether or not it was accompanied by such humiliating rituals as whipping or the placing of the prisoner in fetters and chains (Josephus, *Jewish Antiquities* 18.119, 189-93), likewise connoted disgrace (Plato, *Gorgias*, 525 a-b; Antiphon, *Speeches*, 5.18; Demosthenes, *Against Timocrates*, 24.87, 125; cf. Demosthenes, *Epistles*, 2.17; Acts 5.41) because the lack of freedom and such bodily abuses—where narrated—were normally associated with enslaved persons. Trials or judicial procedures could also be viewed as public spectacles, as Seneca attests (*Epistles*, 14.2). Such rituals of contempt or degradation—like flogging, dismemberment, and crucifixion—were customarily reserved for the punishment of the enslaved (Diodorus Siculus, *Library of History*, 5.38.1; Seneca, *De ira*, 3.24.32; Josephus, *Jewish War* 7.203; Dorotheus, *Carmen astrologicum*, 5.36; Dio Cassius, *Roman History*, 49.12.4; Plautus, *Mostellaria*, 56; Plautus, *Miles gloriosus*, 359-60). A public execution (or capital punishment) demonstrated, therefore, not only the violent power of the adjudicating authorities but also their attempt to stage the humiliation of the condemned person as a public spectacle (Coleman 1990).

Mark does not shy away from a graphic presentation of the rituals of contempt associated with Jesus' death. The whole of Mk 15.1-39 may be divided into three scenes of shame: a formal trial or interrogation scene in which Jesus is charged as a king by Pilate who (after having Jesus whipped) hands him over to soldiers to be crucified (15.1-15); a mock drama scene in which the soldiers pretend to honor Jesus as a king even while they abuse and strip him of the purple cloak first given to him as a royal garment (15.16-20); and the crucifixion proper in which Jesus faces his last hours sentenced as a king not appointed by Rome, and thus having to endure the public humiliating death of crucifixion by which Rome punished political rebels (15.21-39).

Earlier, Mark presents the gruesome killing of John whose truth-telling work and witness had eventuated in a beheading at the hands of a provincial collaborator with Rome, Herod Antipas (6.17-29). Mark dwells on the gruesome details of John's death—the dinner-time execution, the gory death by beheading, the arrival of the decapitated head of John the Baptist on a platter—to show the harsh, stark reality of Roman violence faced by a truth-telling representative, John (6.14-29). In the case of Jesus, whose death would come at the hands of one of Rome's direct representatives, the procurator Pilate, Mark speeds most of the Gospel along but adjusts the pace of the narrative's closing scenes to highlight the devastating crucible of suffering that Jesus faced—the day by day and then hour by hour travesty of justice that leads to his final cries of pain from a shameful cross on a dark day. Mark makes no attempts to sanitize crucifixion, to embroider Jesus' death with the Roman political correctness of cry-less courage, Stoic *apatheia* (i.e. disengagement or freedom from human emotions), and heroic indifference (Bowersock 1994: 55-76). No, Jesus cries, and he cries loudly; and the nails, and the crown of thorns, and the incessant mockeries are all there so as not to erase the horrific violence with which Rome worked its acts of terror upon a man bereft of even a single, loyal friend.

Mark's depiction of Pilate, moreover, is not that of an innocuous governor. Markan auditors would not easily dismiss from the imagination the sight of a bound Jesus (15.1) repeatedly called a 'king' by Pilate (15.2, 9, 12). A 'king' in chains is a king humiliated. Thus, before the soldiers offer up a mock king drama, Pilate's interrogation—presented in the presence of the chief priests—is also a scene of shame. Worse yet, although Pilate knows Jesus to have been handed over out of envy (15.10), he not only delivers Jesus over to the soldiers for crucifixion but also humiliates this staged 'king' with a whipping (15.15).

The mockery that began with Pilate was sustained through the brief mock enthronement play (15.16-20) preceding the crucifixion. Led away for execution, the soldiers first orchestrate a parody of Jesus as a king. They dress Jesus in purple, a color associated with royalty. They offer him a crown, hail him as king of the Jews, and offer him a mock scepter (cf. Mic. 5.1 (LXX 4.14) that is used to strike him on the head (15.17-19a). Humiliating him with their spit, they then kneel down as if to show him reverence (15.19b). All of this twisted, tyrannical game comes to a royal end when the soldiers take off the purple robe and put Jesus' own clothes on him again (15.20). Thus, each change of garments (from Jesus' own clothes to the purple garment and again to his own clothes) signifies a change in status all at the hands and mercy of Pilate's henchmen (Marcus 2006: 82).

Beyond Pilate's interrogation and the soldiers' royal parody, Mark continues the emphasis on mockery through the crucifixion itself (15.21-39). The whole scene, which exposes the commentary of onlookers, is yet another venue in which Jesus as a staged king is shamed. It should be noted that Jesus is never specifically called a 'king' in this Gospel until Mark 15, where he receives the appellation six times (Marcus 2006: 73). For Marcus, the designation of Jesus as a king, told by the narrator but attributed to the Roman executioners, was a specific type of mockery, namely, a parody directed against one who—from the perspectives of the Romans—deemed himself to have a higher status than he, in fact, had (2006: 79-80). Marcus notes, for example, the Romans' typical talionic punishment, that is, the punishment of a person on the basis of their perception of the type of crime of which the person was guilty (2006: 81). Fraudulent persons might have their hands amputated while co-adulterers could be burned alive together (Marcus 2006: 81). Death by crucifixion, thus, could parody the assumed overweening exaltation of the convicted, with some crosses lifted high or higher than usual to mark vertically the overweening of the convicted person (Marcus 2006: 79-80). Crucifixion, in effect, was a rejection of the presumed status of the convicted person, at least in the eyes of the Romans.

So, the Romans mock the presumed status of Jesus at every turn. He who is called a king is too weak to carry his own cross and thus the soldiers conscript Simon of Cyrene (or modern-day Libya, 15.21). The king is stripped of his own possessions over which others fight to see who would take what (15.24; cf. Ps. 22.18). The king is mocked with the title of the placard 'king of the Jews' (15.26). The king is elevated with two bandits (who conceivably could have been understood as his retinue, 15.15.27; Marcus 2006:

82-84). As a king, he receives the taunts of passersby (15.29), the chief priests and scribes (15.31-32), and the bandits (cf. Isa. 53.12) on either side (15.32). Furthermore, this king is impaled on a cross and presented in the most abject solitary state, with Jesus uttering shrieking cries in his final hours (15.33, 37). The picture drawn here is one thus of utter rejection.

Furnished only with these scenes of shame, Markan auditors would not have had much hope. They would not have wanted to remain in a group so decorously laced with shame and abject degradation. How could they remain in the movement when their leader appeared to have been one of the latter-day victims of Rome's political dominance and authority? Fortunately, these painful scenes of shame are not the totality of Mark's narrative. Mark's 'beginning of the good news' had more to offer. It had a longer story. It also recast some of the shame with prevailing rhetorical strategies for enhancing status.

The Typology of the Prophetic Envoy

By the time Mark's earliest auditors heard that Gospel, a rich and organic prophetic tradition had developed in what we would today call the Hebrew Bible (or Old Testament). That tradition included prophetic history told through narrative material in what now would be called the Pentateuch and the Historical Books (e.g. 1–2 Kings) along with the writing prophets such as Isaiah, Jeremiah, Amos, Jonah and so forth (cf. Aernie 2012: 1-51). Many of the writings of Second Temple Judaism (e.g. the scrolls at Qumran or works composed by writers such as the historian Josephus, the philosopher Philo, and the scribe Ben Sira) responded to the historical circumstances of the later period with allusions to the oracular announcements, power-brokering, or confrontational style of earlier prophets (Aernie 2012: 36-51).

According to Richard Horsley, establishment officials often tried to execute prophets in biblical lore (2003: 90): from Ahab and Jezebel who wanted to kill Elijah (1 Kings 19) to Jehoiakim who wanted to kill Uriah, the son of Shemaiah (Jer. 26.20-23) to the Judean officials who wanted to kill Jeremiah (Jer. 26.7-23). In the case of Jeremiah, moreover, the prophet suffered a myriad of abuses for his relentless pronouncements or judgments. According to Michael Knowles, traditions about Jeremiah—whether in the canonical books we know as Jeremiah and Lamentations or other Second Temple Judaism texts such as 1 Esdras and Josephus's *Jewish Antiquities*—depict him as a rejected prophet: 'Jeremiah is mocked and cursed (Jer. 15.10; 20.7-8), persecuted and plotted against (Jer. 17.18; 18.18; 20.10), beaten and put into stocks (Jer. 20.2; 37.15), imprisoned (Jer. 32.2-3; 33.1; 37.15-16), cast into a cistern (Jer. 38.6), ...and, ultimately, martyred by stoning (*Lives of the Prophets*, 2.1)' (1993: 248).

Yet, prophets, whatever their fates, were deemed as the deity's 'envoys and ambassadors', for such was the role of Israel's prophets (Matthews 2012: 22). As messengers of God, the prophets were portrayed as sent by God or as persons who were given the word of God (Jer. 39.1–40.13). Such a commission as agents of God entitled prophets—whether they received it or not—to the honor of the one sending them. With such pre-existing traditions about a prophetic figure available, then, writers in the biblical world frequently recast the shame-laden depictions of their venerated subjects by appealing to the basic template of prophets. The Book of Acts, for example, portrays the apostles and Paul as prophets despite the shame-laden experiences of these protagonists throughout the narrative. Indeed, experiences of shame dart that narrative. A beating follows a warning (Acts 5.27-40). Stephen, tried on trumped-up charges, ultimately faces the spectacle of a stoning (Acts 6.8–7.60). Saul, stylized as a persecutor, initially seeks to hustle up people who are a part of Jesus' prophetic movement (Acts 9.1-2) before he then begins to suffer the same spectacle-laden horrors. He is stoned (Acts 14.19), beaten more than once (Acts 16.23; cf. 21.32), arrested (Acts 21.33), imprisoned more than once (Acts 16.23; 24.27), and tried (Acts 25.6–26.32). Yet, the Book of Acts never ceases to promote the prophetic (and also philosophical) mettle of the protagonists. The protagonists are drawn like Septuagint prophets. Peter and John (Acts 3.1-10) and later Paul (Acts 14.8-10) heal like the prophets Elijah and Elisha. Stephen's speech both speaks of rejected Septuagint prophets and sets up the dynamics for Stephen's own rejection (Acts 7.1-60). Thus, scenes of shame are recast through the typology of the rejected prophet, an emissary sent by God.

The Teacher Jesus as a Prophet in the Gospel of Mark

Few would doubt that Mark depicts Jesus as a prophet. This is certainly a typology with which Mark begins shortly before Jesus is cast as a disciple-gathering teacher (1.16-20; 2.13-14). Framed by the repetition of diction about the gospel or 'good news' (1.1, 14, 15), the first unit of Mark's Gospel (1.1-15) prepares auditors for the confirmation of John and Jesus as the deity's prophetic brokers. That is, the opening scenes of 1.1-15 create the basic typological grid from which the auditors will form their impressions of the Gospel's principal characters. Thus, the first brushstrokes against the Markan narrative canvas all draw their colors from a prophetic palette. So, John and Jesus are clearly depicted as prophets. Like the Septuagint prophets, they make proclamations (1.4, 7, 14; cf. Joel 4.9; Jon. 1.2; 3.2, 4; Isa. 61.1). Like such prophets, they travel in and around those spaces—like the wilderness and the Jordan—once ingredient to Israel's formation, solidarity, and refuge (Hoffmeier 2005: 37; Funk 1959: 214). Like these earlier prophets, John and Jesus re-enact a prophetic succession tale, a tale in which virtually the end of one prophet's work is quickly followed by virtually the beginning of yet another prophet's work. In fact, the early references to the Spirit near the Jordan river, the 'up-down' imagery, the diction of sight, the repeated references to the heavens, and the 'forty days' reference (1.1-15) all clearly have associations with the prophetic succession episodes of 2 Kings 2 in the Septuagint (Burnett 2010: 281-97; Davis 1984: 384-95; Satterthwaite 1998: 1-28).

The typology of Jesus as a prophet also continues throughout the Gospel. Later, Jesus has disciples (as was true for the prophets Elijah and Elisha; cf. 1 Kgs 19.16, 19-21). Likewise, Jesus heals and raises a child from the dead (also in the Elijah and Elisha tradition; cf.1 Kgs 17.17-24; 2 Kgs 4.8-37). Also, some Markan characters identify Jesus on the order of prophets in 6.14-16; 8.27-30, though he is certainly more than just a prophet. Furthermore, Jesus meets two prophets (Moses and Elijah) on the mountain of transfiguration (9.1-13). With many allusions to Elijah/Elisha or Moses for that matter, it would not have been difficult for Mark's earliest auditors to see John and Jesus then as confrontational prophets.

The Teacher Jesus as a Prophetic Envoy in the Gospel of Mark

Critical for this discussion is the recognition that as prophets both John and Jesus should have been received with the honor requisite for agents of God. That is, an unspoken emissary etiquette in the larger society was the expectation that an emissary would receive the honor associated with the one who sent him or her. As Margaret M. Mitchell has explained, the 'proper reception of the envoy necessarily entails the proper reception of the one who sent him' (1992: 645). So, when envoys were not received well or when their authority to act or speak on behalf of the one sending them was not recognized, the dishonor reflected back on the one sending them (Bederman 2001: 95). Thus, when the Ammonite Hanun permitted the shameful acts of shaving half of the beards and cutting off parts of the garments of David's envoys, for example, such acts were, in effect, affronts directed toward king David himself (2 Sam. 10.2-5), with the consequence that a war ensued. As Philo would note in general, 'For whatever ambassadors suffer (*presbeis hypomenōsin*) recoils upon those who sent (*tous pempsantes*) them' (Philo, *Embassy to Gaius* 369).

It is with little wonder then that 'sending' and 'receiving' diction figures heavily into emissary forms of hospitality or inhospitality. Envoys—whether alone or with others—were 'sent' (*empemphthēsan*, cf. Plutarch, *Moralia* 231F; *apostellō*, cf. Gen. 32.4; Num. 22.5; 1 Macc. 8.17; 12.1; and Jer. 30.8 [LXX]; *pempō*, cf. Apollodorus, *Epitome* E.2.13) on behalf of a dispatching party or parties. Furthermore, an envoy or an embassy expected to be 'received' (*hypodechomai*) courteously (Josephus, *Jewish Antiquities* 14.343; cf. Polybius, *Histories* 27.5), or treated with 'hospitality' (*xenia*, Josephus, *Jewish Antiquities* 12.165), and 'heard fully' (*diakouō*, Josephus, *Jewish Antiquities* 20.195). They could be 'welcomed' or 'received' (*epidechomai*) with honor (1 Macc. 12.8). They expected, moreover, not to be detained but to be able to return to the dispatching party (Gen. 32.3-7; Num. 22.5-14).

Mark's diction about sending and reception appears to reflect this emissary etiquette as a critical ingredient for understanding the prophetic roles of John, Jesus, and potentially the disciples. Whatever the referent of the Gospel's opening citation (presumably directed to both John and Jesus because the imperatives that follow are in the plural), the words 'Behold I send (*apostellō*) my messenger' (1.2) prepare the audience to give honor to a character (or characters) sent by God. In Jesus' parable of the Sower and its interpretation (4.3-20), Jesus speaks of the good soil as 'those who hear the word, *welcome* (*paradechomai*) it, and bear fruit' (4.20). When Jesus sends out his own disciples as emissaries (6.6b-13, 30), he warns them that some of the homes to which they are sent might not receive (*dechomai*) them (6.11). This second commission of disciples (the first given in 3.13-19) is given, moreover, in a thematic context about prophetic reception. That is, in the previous episode (6.1-6a), in the setting of a visit to the synagogue at Nazareth, Jesus (who has been followed by his disciples, 6.1) warns: 'A prophet is not without honor except in his own hometown and among his own fellow kinspeople, and in his own house' (6.4). Then, in the subsequent episode (which includes flashback scenes and references to prophets), Mark's earliest auditors learn about the death of the prophet John the baptizer (6.14-29). In later reflections to his disciples, Jesus also avers: 'Whoever welcomes (*dechomai*) one such child in my name welcomes (*dechomai*) me, and whoever welcomes (*dechomai*) me welcomes (*dechomai*) not me but the one who sent (*apostellō*) me' (9.37).

Mark and the Parable of the Dishonored Emissaries

Mark's most critical use of emissary etiquette, however, is saved for Mark's second largest parable, the parable of the Tenants or what could be called the parable of the Dishonored Emissaries. Indeed, the parable reinforces some of the larger Gospel's themes (sending, suffering of messengers, the beloved son, and his death). In addition, the parable also provides information about the back-story of the Gospel (cf. 12.1 and Isa. 5.1-7) and about the events that will occur off of the narrative stage when the story concludes (12.9). That the words 'stone' and 'builders' (12.10; 13.1-2) are found in association with the parable's application and with the prophetic and apocalyptic farewell discourse (13.2-37) also encourages the Markan auditors to pay attention to it (Tolbert 1996: 237). Given that the parable's application is directed at Jesus' opposition (12.12), presumably the same persons who have asked Jesus about his authority, the parable also prepares the Markan auditors for the inevitability of Jesus' death by that same implacable opposition (cf. 11.18; 14.43).

Mark's framing of Jesus' death within the context of the second longest parable of the narrative suggests then that the death is a signal of the immediacy of God's final consummation of divine reigning. That parable depicts the patience of God in sending one messenger after another to bring back some of the fruit of the Lord's vineyard only to have the messengers treated with contempt and, in some cases, with violence. The critique of contempt may have been at the heart of Jesus' harsh words for the temple establishment if Mark's auditors knew the 'abominations' context in which the Jer. 7.11 allusion was cast (cf. Jer. 7.10). Clearly, dishonor is leveled at the 'final' (*eschaton*, 12.6) messenger when he is killed despite his status, that is, as the heir of the Lord's vineyard and as the 'beloved son', the very language used to describe Jesus at his baptism (1.11) and at his transfiguration (9.7). With the death—indeed murder—of the heir, however, the Lord of the vineyard will no longer have patience with the rituals of humiliation leveled against the deity's emissaries. Rather, God will vent wrath, destroy (or put out of business) those failing to produce fruit, and give the vineyard to others. Mark's placement of this parable in a section of the Gospel that repeatedly mentions the temple seems to indicate that Mark expected the demise of the temple leaders and, as Mk 13.1-2 makes clear, the destruction of the temple itself. More than that, however, Mark understood the death of the last principal emissary to be the catalyst for the consummation of God's rule.

What is also clear from the parable is the authorization of those who were sent, that is, all of the emissaries. The parable certainly supports the authorization of the beloved son (12.6). Indeed, the stone that was rejected or refused (12.10-11; cf. Ps 118.22-23 [117.22-23, LXX]) by the builders—presumably that beloved son—is exalted as the 'elevated cornerstone' (Marcus 2009: 808). Yet, the repetition of the sending diction certifies the action of all those sent to do their job: to request some of the fruit from the owner's vineyard. The parable then reiterates a key theme of Mark's Gospel, namely, the rejection of God's emissaries. The hope of the parable, though, is that the contemptuous assault on the emissaries has reached a turning point because the divine patron, after the murder of the beloved Son, will 'give' (*didōmi*) the vineyard to others (12.9). Readers then can expect—at least on the other side of the narrative stage—for a time when those who now are in charge of the vineyard will no longer hold sway over it. That good news is *about* Jesus, *for* his followers, and *against* those who have dishonored God's emissaries.

Summary

Mark thus recasts its principle characters as prophetic emissaries. Whatever troubles portend for them—a beheading for John, a cross for Jesus, rejection and more for the disciples (13.9-13), their sordid scenes of shame are read as the expected travails of rejection that prophets—especially confrontational prophets—could face. The sting of shame, however, is lessened because John, Jesus, and sometimes the disciples seem to follow the destiny of a venerable script from Israel's own sacred traditions. In recasting the shame, Mark depicts Jesus' death as a dishonor that is directed not solely to Jesus but to the one who sent him, that is, to God. Mark thus reads Jesus' death as an affront, a breach of emissary etiquette. The type of death (death by crucifixion) is not as critical here except in the conventional sphere of how it would have been regarded. What matters for the Markan author is how the death looks to God. As we shall eventually see, this perspective— how the death looks to God—will also explain why the Gospel is simply 'the beginning of the good news of Jesus Christ' (1.1). There is more news underway as a result of the death of the heir of the Lord of the vineyard, the last principal prophetic emissary (12.1-9). Mark's story is only the beginning of that good news.

Chapter 4

JESUS AS A POWERFUL BROKER

Introduction

Mark's story about Jesus as a teacher is replete with instances of indignity, moments of mockery, and scenes of shame. Throughout the Gospel, Jesus faces shame-ridden moments of one sort or another: by those who question his authority near the beginning (2.7, 10) or ending of the Gospel (11.28, 33); by scribes who come down from Jerusalem to assign Jesus' power to diabolical forces (3.22); by on-and-quickly-off-again-wailers who deride Jesus with laughter (5.38-40); and even among the home-town crowd in a synagogue at Nazareth, where Jesus laments the fate of all prophets ('A prophet is not without honor except in his own country and among his own kin and in his own house', 6.1-6a, esp. 6.4, NRSV).

Yet, most of the scenes of shame appear near the end of the Gospel. As Jesus states in his first passion/resurrection prediction, he will be rejected by the established provincial authorities, that is, he will be reckoned as worthless (*apodokimazō*, 8.31), the very opposite of being approved (*dokimazō*). As he states in his second passion/resurrection prediction, he also will be 'handed over' or 'delivered up' (*paradidōmi*) into the hands of people. As we have seen, Mark's repetition of *paradidōmi* diction connotes a negative thematic tone that Mark's earliest auditors would easily connect with shame. In Jesus' third passion/resurrection prediction, most of the verbs mark the coming moments as shameful scenes of powerlessness. While Jesus and others 'will go up' into Jerusalem (with *anabainomen* being an active voice verb, 10.33a), the Son of the Human One (or the Son of Man) will be handed over (with *paradothēsetai* being a passive voice verb, 10.33b). With the exception of the last verb ('he will arise'), the subsequent verbs of the prediction clauses all mark not what the Son of the Human One will do, but what will happen to him: the established provincial authorities will condemn him to death and will deliver him up to the Gentiles, and the Gentiles will deride him, mock him, and whip him (10.33c-34).

Then as now, spitting on another was an affront associated with shame (Deut. 25.9; cf. Num. 12.14; Isa. 50.6). Also, corporal punishment of any kind—such as whipping—signified the humiliation and helplessness perceived to be associated with the enslaved (Roller 2001: 221). Thus, all of these actions were compounded forms of indignity designed to make a person appear powerless before Rome or its indirect or direct representatives.

Yet, more indignities are also registered as Mark narrates the actual day of Jesus' execution. As if a mock king drama (15.16-20), wagging heads (a well-known sign of contempt, 15.29; cf. Job 16.4; Jer. 18.16; 2 Kgs 19.21; Lam. 2.15; Pss. 22.7; 109.25), the reproach of those crucified with him (15.32), and corrosive speech about Jesus' inability to save himself or of his need for someone to come to help him (15.31, 36) were not shameful enough, a key goal of the humiliating violence of crucifixion itself was to indicate the absolute powerlessness of the crucified person, and, as a corollary, the absolute power of Rome.

This was Rome's objective, for example, when a Roman general crucified 6,000 enslaved persons after the suppression of the revolt led by Spartacus in 71 BCE (veritably the most horrific example of Rome's brutal power recorded in the annals of the period; see Appian, *Roman Civil Wars*, 1.120). Such was also Rome's objective when its legate of Syria responded to Judean resistance against the Romans by crucifying 2,000 Jews while negotiations about the division of the kingdom of Herod I (4 BCE) were taking place (Josephus, *Jewish War* 2.5.2 §75; *Jewish Antiquities* 17.10.10 §295). Such was also Rome's objective when Titus and the Roman legions scourged (*mastigoō*) and crucified (*anastauroō*) up to 500 Jews each day, which was a horrific instance of Roman violence against the Judeans as captured by the historian Josephus's coverage of the Jewish-Roman war of 66–70 CE (*Jewish War* 5.449-50). When one adds many other crucifixions of Judeans, Samaritans, and Galileans (Tiberius Alexander's crucifixion of James and Simon, the sons of Judas of Gamala; the Syrian legate Quadratus's crucifixion of Samaritans and Judeans; and Governor Florus's crucifixion of Jerusalemites; cf. Horsley 2011: 181-82), one must agree with Richard Horsley's summary about the power dynamics of crucifixion. 'There can be no question that in first-century Judea and Galilee crucifixion was a Roman form of execution used to punish and intimidate' (Horsley 2011: 182).

Given how such scenes of shame were associated with powerlessness, the Gospel of Mark repeatedly depicts Jesus as a powerful broker. Jesus is not a teacher of words alone. Mark constantly features Jesus as a man of power. On the one hand, Mark does not deny Roman power as exercised through Rome's indirect power brokers such as the Herodians and the established provincial elites and a direct power-broker such as Pilate. On the other hand, Mark squarely positions Jesus as a man entrusted with significant power. Jesus' powerful brokerage status thus discounts the notion that Jesus was a helpless, powerless victim of Rome's intimidation politics even as his own Septuagint-based brokerage style contrasts with the brokerage politics of Rome and its representatives.

To demonstrate Mark's deployment of the typology of a powerful broker, this chapter will first define brokerage and indicate the diction of brokerage that Mark's earliest auditors would likely have recognized as the parlance of power distribution. Next, the chapter will illustrate how Mark deploys such diction in its descriptions of the teacher Jesus and some of his followers. Finally, the chapter will expose how Mark's Gospel contrasts two types of brokerage. On the one hand, Mark acknowledges the tyrannical brokerage styles of Herod Antipas and Pilate. On the other hand, Mark contrasts that tyrannical style with the brokerage of Jesus, a style informed greatly by two Septuagint typologies of mediation: the New Exodus Liberator and the Danielic Son of the Human One. In presenting this contrast, Mark resolves what could otherwise have been understood as a conundrum, namely, the narrative's shift from demonstrations of a powerful broker to a presentation of a suffering teacher.

Brokerage in the Ancient Mediterranean World

In the ancient Mediterranean, a broker was a person authorized to mediate the distribution of power, possessions, or peace between a patron on the one hand and the patron's client or clients on the other. As Douglas Edwards has noted, 'local elites across the Greek East played key roles in serving as the representatives who brokered power relations between the divine, regional, and local power' (1996: 94). Yet, claims of brokerage power were at times contested as varying affiliated groups—from the local elites and the high-ranking officials of cities and regions to associations that provided venues for commensality, honor, and burial to those deemed as prophetic figures—jostled against each other in various 'webs of power' (Edwards 1996: 12; Ascough 2008: 33-45; McRae 2011: 170-75).

A key expression used then to describe the brokering process was the word *exousia* ('authority'). *Exousia*, the virtual center of a constellation of diction to indicate brokerage arrangements, was often deployed when claims were made about the legitimate right for one party to mediate between two other parties. After the death of Antiochus IV, when Demetrius I and Alexander I Epiphanes rivaled each other for Antiochus's throne, for example, Demetrius I gave authority (*edōken exousian*) to the Maccabean Jonathan (1 Macc. 10.6) to gather together a force. Years later, Antiochus VI Epiphanes, the son of Alexander I Epiphanes, both confirmed Jonathan's priesthood and gave authority to Jonathan to drink from gold cups and to don purple (1 Macc. 11.58). 1 Maccabees also speaks of persons 'having authority' (*echō exousian*), or, in this instance, of Demetrius I presumably declaring that no one else would have authority over the Jewish nation.

Likewise, Epictetus, as told by his student Arrian, deployed the images of either giving authority (1.29.11; 2.13) or having authority (*Discourses*

1.25.2; 1.29.50, 52; 2.2.26; 2.13.14, 23; 3.24.48,70; 4.1.59, 60, 61 [twice], 82; 4.7.10,17; 4.10.29-30 [twice]; 4.12.9). Josephus also speaks of several rulers who either had the authority to grant a position of power (such as a vice-regency or a kingship) and those who gave authority to other rulers to do so. Joseph, for example, was 'given authority' (*exousias...dotheisēs*) by Pharaoh to be robed in purple (*Jewish Antiquities* 2.90.5.7). With the expression 'giving authority' (*dontas...exousian*), Josephus avers that Antony recognized Herod I as a king (*Jewish Antiquities* 15.76), as did Julius Caesar (*Jewish War* 1.474). Likewise, in reference to Herod I, Josephus also speaks of Caesar allowing Herod to have the 'authority' (*exousia*) to dispose of his kingdom and to appoint (literally 'to seat') a successor (*Jewish Antiquities* 16.129; cf. 17.233). Similarly, with the expression *exousian ... paradidōmi*, Josephus acknowledged Julius Caesar's approval of Herod's authority to give over his throne to one of his successors at his death (*Jewish Antiquities* 16.92; cf. *didōmi exousian*, 17.240; 17.313). Josephus also notes that Julius Caesar alone was able 'to grant the authority' (*didōmi tēn exousian*) of kingship to Archelaus, Herod's son (*Jewish Antiquities* 17.239, 313; cf. 16.365).

Other expressions in the constellation of brokerage terms also included 'request' (*aiteō*) diction, 'deeds' (*poieō*) diction, and power (*dynamis*) diction. One thus could ask or 'make a request' (*aiteō*) for 'gifts' (*dōrea*, Plutarch, *Demosthenes*, 8). One could also request (*aiteō*) a powerful figure to 'make' (*poieō*) a position for a third party (Josephus, *Jewish War* 1.483; cf. 1.282), or mandate that a request be made and then offer the requested item as a gift (Josephus, *Jewish War* 11.57; *Jewish Antiquities* 18.289-97). Furthermore, one could have power (might or ability) to do something or one could have power (rule or control, cf. 2 Macc. 13.2) over something. One's power or ability then is demonstrated through one's acts (Ps 144.4 LXX) or one's deeds (1 Kgs 16.5; 2 Kgs 13.8; 14.28).

The Markan Teacher and his Students as Powerful Brokers

Within such 'webs of power', Jesus and his followers were seen by many as emissary brokers sent from God. According to Alan B. Wheatley, 'His [Jesus'] brokering operated with regard to an emerging moment in the favor of God, a sphere of contingent sovereignty, announced as the Kingdom of God. Jesus and his followers were seen to provide access to benefits within the favor of God, and so to fulfill the promises made by the latter through prior servants, the prophets' (2011: 13).

Mark depicts Jesus as such an emissary broker. Cognates of the word *exousia* pervade the narrative landscape of Mark's Gospel. Nominal cognates are found in 1.27; 2.10; 3.15; 6.7; 11.28 (twice), 29, 33; and 13.34. A verbal cognate in compound form (*katexousiazō*, 'lord it over') is also found in 10.42. Yet, the expression *exousia* itself is difficult to define in Mark, with some interpreters linking it to 'power' (which might be implied given that Jesus' comments on forgiveness seem to be directed at the thoughts of the scribes who have questioned whether anyone other than God has the ability (*dynamai*) to forgive sins (2.7), while other interpreters link the term to 'legitimacy' or 'freedom', which could mesh well with the term *exesti*, the impersonal verb related to the noun *exousia*, that is often translated as 'it is permissible' or 'it is lawful' (cf. Mark 2.24, 26; 3.4; 6.18; 10.2; 12.14; cf. Dillon 1995: 97).

One clear indicator of Mark's use of the brokerage parlance is that Mark repeatedly speaks of persons 'having authority' (1.22; cf.1.27; 3.15) or 'giving authority' (6.7). With such diction, Mark describes both Jesus and the disciples as having an authority given to them by a higher figure. With such authority, both Jesus and his students are marked as teachers in word and deed who embody a philosophical ideal (Seneca, *Epistles*, 52.8-9; Philo, *Life of Moses*, 2.209-16; Dio Chrysostom, *Discourses* 72.1; Maximus of Tyre, *Discourses* 1).

The Teacher Jesus as an Authorized Powerful Broker
In the case of Jesus, we are first told about his *exousia* when he was teaching in a synagogue in Capernaum (1.21-28). Mark notes that Jesus was teaching as one having authority and not as the scribes (1.22). Such a statement is the Gospel's perspective on power arrangements, that is, the Gospel's claims about Jesus' legitimate right compared to others who may have been deemed as established brokers. The Gospel's argument is that Jesus' stylized opponents—in this case, the scribes (though they are only now being introduced and not actually presented on the narrative stage)—were not authorized by the only source of power with whom the Markan Jesus has been identified, that is, with the deity. Jesus, by virtue of his status as son (1.11; cf. perhaps 1.1), has authority (or has been given authority) by that source to demand the obedience of unclean spirits. In effect, while the Markan deity has the ultimate authority or dominion over such spirits, the deity has given authority or dominion to Jesus who then also has authority or dominion over the unclean spirits. Thus, like subjects under a ruler, the demons are obliged to obey Jesus. So, although many in Mark's world would see Rome as the key determinant for the mediation of *exousia* or dominion, Mark insists that such mediation belongs only and properly so to the deity.

As one of the deity's authorized agents, Jesus has not only authority over spirits but also authority to forgive sins (or release persons from obligations, 2.10). In fact, Mark continues to spell out Jesus' dominion even if the expression *exousia* is not used. As we have noted earlier, lexical links between 1.21-28 and 4.35-41, for example, bespeak Jesus' dominion over the 'sea'. Subsequent miracles in 5.1-43 indicate furthermore that Jesus also has dominion over demonic forces in foreign places as well as over sick-ness and death. This teacher then is a powerful broker. Power (*dynamis*) terms in the first half of the Markan narrative (6.2, 14; 9.39) and a flurry of miracles themselves indicate Jesus' power or the power of select follow-ers of Jesus or others acting in his name. Furthermore, Jesus is presented as a teacher who can get things done. Told to declare what God 'has done' (*poieō*, 5.19) in having mercy on him, the Gerasene declares what Jesus 'has done' (*poieō*, 5.20). Jesus' ability to 'make' (*poieō*) those who cannot hear to hear and those who cannot speak to speak leads villagers to declare that Jesus 'has done' (*poieō*) all things well (7.37). Even if Jesus is not able 'to do' (*poieō*) a power or a miracle (lit. a 'power', *dynamis*) in some places (6.5), he is not incapable of distributing the heavenly patron's power. Mark simply wants to indicate the link between power and faith (6.6; cf. 9.19-29).

Beyond 1.21-28 and 2.1-12, other sections of Mark's Gospel will revisit the issue of Jesus' authority to mediate the supreme benefactor's power, pos-sessions, or peace. Scribes from Jerusalem, for example, assign the power behind Jesus' works to Beelzebul (3.20-30), though Jesus refuted their logic by showing that his efforts worked against Beelzebul and were neither for Beelzebul nor for his house/kingdom/rule (3.23-27). Toward the end of the Gospel, when Jesus is in Jerusalem, the scribes, chief priests, and elders ask Jesus about his authority: 'By what authority do you do these things? Or who gave you authority to do these things?' (11.28). Refusing initially to tell them the source of his authority (11.29, 33) because they refused to declare whether John's baptism was from heaven or of humans, Jesus actu-ally reveals the source of his authority (and John's) in a parable (the parable of the Tenants [or the parable of the Dishonored Emissaries], 12.1-12). The parable repeatedly uses *apostellō* ('I send') expressions (12.2-6) to indi-cate God as the source of all prophetic ministries, including that of God's 'beloved son' (12.6).

The Teacher's Students as Authorized Powerful Brokers
In two formal commissioning scenes, Mark makes clear that Jesus' disci-ples are also authorized to be powerful brokers. When growing needs (3.7-12) demand that Jesus enlist others to assist him (3.13-19), he formally selects twelve that he 'might send' (*apostellō*, 3.14). They, too, embrace a word and deed ideal. They are not sent out only to make a proclamation but to have authority to cast out demons as well. In the second formal com-mission (6.7b-13, 30), when Jesus began 'to send' (*apostellō*) his disciples two by two (6.7), the disciples maintain the word and deed ideal. They pro-claim that all persons should repent (6.12; cf. 1.4, 15, 38, 39). Yet, they are also given authority over the unclean spirits (6.7). So, they cast out many demons and heal (6.13). When they return, they report all that they did (*poieō*) and taught (*didaskō*, 6.30).

Thus, both Jesus and his disciples are powerful brokers. They are not teachers in words alone but in actions or works of power as well. Yet, the disciples do not always fare well as brokers in Mark's Gospel. Instead, as the Gospel advances its narrative, the disciples seem to follow a different brokerage script. Perhaps the disciples are stylized as bad brokers so that Mark may contrast the Septuagint-based brokerage style of Jesus with that of Rome's representatives and any others who are sometimes seduced to follow such representatives.

The Gospel of Mark and Contrasting Styles of Brokerage

As the Gospel of Mark develops, Jesus shifts from calling disciples and commissioning disciples to correcting them. He must attempt to correct the disciples because they appear to be influenced by the 'leaven' of the Pharisees and the 'leaven' of Herod, presumably representing some improper values (8.15). His followers appear to be blind to the values they will need to prepare them for the crucible (11.1–16.8). The whole of the 'bread' and 'blindness' sections of 6.31–10.52, then, provide a space in which Mark contrasts brokerage styles. Markan auditors learn about the brokerage style of Herod and others who seek to throw their weight around. In carefully orchestrated episodes of comparison and contrast, Markan auditors learn about Jesus' Septuagint-based brokerage. For Mark, Jesus' brokerage style is the only one that will prepare disciples to face the inevitable shame-ridden crucibles that will come to their lives. The 'bread' and 'blindness' sections then are designed to point ahead to the inevitable discomforts of the Jerusalem scenes. If Mark's auditors can learn to correct their own values, they will be ready for the litany of shame-ridden experiences cast in the peristasis catalogue or 'hardship list' of 13.9-13. If they do not learn to correct their own values, the end for them will be similar to the end for the disciples: failure in the face of Rome's brokering authorities.

Lording it over Others: Rome and its Brokerage Style

We may begin with the brokerage style that the Gospel critiques, namely, the brokerage style of Rome's representatives. Rome communicated its power through a network of alliances by means of which it sought to maintain hegemony over its provinces. When Rome's wars of conquest increased the city's peninsular and overseas territorial acquisitions and imperial projects across the republic and the Principate periods, Rome sustained its hegemony through native elite brokers (the upper class order outside of Rome also known as the decurions) who administered the provinces or other territories subject to Roman domination. Rome not only authorized such elites and honored their brokerage loyalty through *beneficia* but also greatly opposed any provincial rulers not recognized by Rome (Tacitus, *Histories*

5.9). Such authorized native elites included the local magistrates or town council members who collected taxes, maintained public order, and administered civilian policing for minor offenses (Fuhrmann 2012: 9, 58-61). Some native elites were also known as friendly monarchs, as with Herod I and some of his descendants. All such elite brokers carefully guarded their status, looked for opportunities to advance themselves or their families in the larger realm of Rome's territorial dominance, and replicated Rome's values through the beneficence networks they established with their own communities and occasionally through the brutal repressive measures with which they ruled.

Mark's audiences were certainly familiar with such provincial brokers. If they did not know directly about Herod I (who built at least three prominently placed imperial temples in first-century BCE Palestine) or his son Archelaus, whose tyrannical postures were frequently noted by the historian Josephus (*Jewish Antiquities* 16.153; 17.304, 342; cf. *Jewish War* 2.84.3-4; *Jewish Antiquities* 17.233), they at least knew of Antipas, Archelaus's brother (cf. Peppard 2011: 92). They knew that Antipas was appointed as a broker over Galilee by Rome. They also knew that he was cruel toward the prophetic emissary John, for Antipas subjected John to a series of humiliating acts: arrest, imprisonment, and a meal-time execution (Mk 6.14-29; cf. Josephus, *Jewish Antiquities* 118.116-17). As I have shown elsewhere, Mark's description of Herod Antipas's rashness, fear, and meal-time libidinal excesses would have placed this so-called 'king' squarely in the mold of a tyrant (Smith 2006).

Likewise, Mark's earliest audiences would have known about other power-brokers such as the scribes (the legal exegetes and judicial experts of the day). At the least, they are portrayed in Mark's Gospel as one of several groups that repetitively questioned Jesus about the implications of his brokerage statements or actions. They question his claim to be able to forgive sins, as if this prerogative did not belong to him (2.1-12). Some of them from Jerusalem attributed the source of his brokerage power to Beelzebul (though they were not able to deny that Jesus was able to cast out demons, 3.22). Present at the scene when Jesus disrupts the temple precincts, scribes along with others seek to put Jesus out of business (11.18). And, again, with other power-brokers, they later question the source of Jesus' brokerage authority (*exousia*, 11.27-33). While not all of the scribes are painted with the same stripe in Mark's Gospel (see 12.28-34), the mentality of most of the group as stylized by Mark is characterized by an open quest for attention and honor for themselves (12.38-40) while also seeking through stealth (14.1) to end the fortunes of anyone who might disturb the stability of their power base with Rome (14.43, 53-64; 15.1). If Mark's audiences knew anything at all about the quick and deadly assaults of Rome's other representatives on those who dared to speak out against the temple (cf. Josephus,

navigation"4. *Jesus as a Powerful Broker*   63

Jewish War 1.651), they would easily see the scribes (who were a part of the Sanhedrin provincial hegemony) as brokers with a vested interest in maintaining control over and respect for the temple even if evidence against Jesus (to support the claim that he vowed to destroy the temple) had to be manufactured on the spot (cf. 14.53-64).

Mark's earliest audiences were also familiar with brokers that Rome directly appointed to serve in its provinces, such as Pilate, the governor of Judea from 26 to 36/37 CE. While most of what we know about Pilate actually comes from Mark and other canonical Christian accounts (Mk 15.1-15, 43-45; Mt. 27.2-25, 58, 62-65; Lk. 3.1; 13.1; 23.1-25, 52; Jn 18.28–19.16, 38; Acts 3.13; 4.27; 13.28; cf. 1 Tim. 6.13), both Philo (in his *Embassy to Gaius*, 301-302) and Josephus (in *Jewish Antiquities* 18.3.1; 18.4.1-2; and *Jewish War* 2.9.2-4) portray Pilate as obstinate and insensitive toward the Jews. Mark's audience certainly knew about Pilate, for under Pilate's authority as a governor appointed by Rome, Jesus was turned over to Roman soldiers for crucifixion (15.1-15). As I have also argued elsewhere, the Gospel of Mark no less portrays Pilate in the same tyrannical garb used to describe Herod Antipas, that is, as a tyrant (Smith 2006). Both rulers overlook issues of justice in order to satisfy the whims of others. In the instance of Pilate, moreover, the clear innocence of Jesus does not provide a dam strong enough to hold back the tide of humiliating cruelties that Pilate allowed the Roman soldiers to unleash. The soldiers whipped Jesus; they mocked him as a king; they beat him in the head and spat upon him. Lastly, they crucified him (15.15-20). While all of these cruelties are exacted on Jesus, Barabbas, a man known for insurrectionary activity, by contrast, is purportedly simply released (15.7, 15), as if irrational and whimsical forces rather than reason and justice governed Pilate's decisions.

Thus, Mark's earliest auditors would have reckoned Rome's brokers as tyrants, as persons who 'lorded it over' (*katexousiazō*, 10.42) others, as persons who used their authority to throw their weight around. The Markan Jesus sees this brokerage style as typical of the Gentiles and warns his disciples: 'But it should not be so among you' (10.42).

A Liberating and Lasting Power: Jesus' Septuagint-Based Brokering Style
By contrast, Mark also presents the brokerage style of Jesus, a style drawn from the Septuagint. In fact, two salient features of Jesus' own brokerage style reflect the Septuagint. On the one hand, Jesus' power is *liberating*. He uses his power to re-enact deeds that were a part of the liberating repertoire of God's earlier acts in history. As a liberator, Jesus enlists followers to join him in a New Exodus 'way' movement against Satan's hostile take-overs of bodies and values. On the other hand, Jesus' power is *lasting*. Although it may appear that Jesus' power was temporally limited, especially as the Gospel depicts him as the passive victim of a series of humiliating acts,

Mark repeatedly associates Jesus with the Danielic Son of the Human One, a trans-temporal agent whose arrival vindicates the unending nature of Jesus' power.

Mark expresses the liberating nature of Jesus' brokerage style through typological allusions to Second Isaiah's New Exodus way. The first signs that the brokerage style of Jesus will depend on Second Isaiah's New Exodus theme appear as early as Mk 1.1-15. That is, the particular prophetic palette with which Mark begins (1.1-15) makes specific intertextual links with the prophet (Second) Isaiah's New Exodus theme. As scholars have long noted, Mk 1.2-3 is not exclusively derived from Isaiah. Instead, it is a conflation of several scriptural texts (cf. Exod. 23.20 LXX, Mal. 3.1, and Isa. 40.3). Still, Second Isaiah's New Exodus theme emphatically resonates within the whole of Mk 1.1-15. So, beyond Mark's specific reference to Isa. 40.3 ('a voice crying in the wilderness', Mk 1.3), Mark's repeated use of *euangelion* (1.1, 15) could signal an allusion to Second Isaiah, for the term was a key part of the New Exodus theme of Isaiah 40–55 (Pao 2000: 32).

Furthermore, Mark's repetition of the word 'way' (*hodos*, 1.2-3), which itself is a key word in the context of each of the three aforementioned conflated texts (including the one from Isaiah), likely alludes to the 'way' theme that Second Isaiah repeatedly evokes from the first exodus (Exod. 13.21; 23.20) to make a case for a second one (Isa. 42.16; 43.16, 19; 48.17; 51.10). Mark's opening scenes also repeat the word 'wilderness' (*erēmos*), which frequently appears in Second Isaiah (40.3; 43.19; 48.20-21; 51.3). Thus, just as Second Isaiah argues that God will restore God's people and lead them through a wilderness way toward a second liberation [from Babylon to Jerusalem] on the order of the first exodus, Mark's earliest scenes seem to allude to this prophetic palette to highlight yet again the deity's ability to bring liberation to those who now hear and believe the gospel (1.15). Finally, Mark's intertextual link with Mal. 3.1 ('Behold, I send my messenger') is itself a link to Isaiah 40 because the messenger in Mal. 3.1 apparently recalls 'Isaiah 40, where a figure in the divine Council is told to prepare the way in the wilderness' (Collins 2007: 216).

Beyond the Markan Opening (1.1-15), Mark's interest in a journey theme continues both in the notices in which Jesus or Jesus and his followers travel *by* sea—or actually by an inland, freshwater lake (1.16; 2.13; 3.7; 4.1, 35; 5.1, 13, 21; 6.45; cf. 6.48-49; 8.10; 8.22; cf. France 2002: 95)—and *into* wilderness areas, as they do in some of the earlier parts of the Gospel, and the travel notices in which Jesus and his followers travel by land or on the 'way' (8.27; 9.33; 9.34; 10.17; 10.32; 10.52), as they do in the later parts of the story.

For many scholars, then, on the one hand, Mark's repetition of the word 'way' (*hodos*) or journey is reminiscent of the first exodus' 'way' (Exod. 13.21; 23.20), the journey through which the ancient Israelites were led from Egypt to liberation (Matthews 2012: 179-80). On the other hand, that 'way' was also like the 'new exodus' of [Second] Isaiah, that is, Isaiah 40–55 (cf. Watts 2000: 80). Thus, as a New Exodus teacher, Jesus leads his followers through a series of water-crossings and in wilderness sojourns before traveling with them on the 'way' to Jerusalem. Mark's journey motif, though, does not solely reveal Jesus' power to reenact the liberating acts of God. Mark's special 'bread' and 'blindness' sections reveal that Mark also seeks to expose the New Exodus values that Jesus' followers should be learning along the way. Satan has taken over not only bodies but also minds or ways of thinking. So, even some of Jesus' followers must correct their ways of thinking. The whole of the Markan journey motif in 1.16–10.52, thus, prepares Jesus' followers to learn the New Exodus values that will be necessary if they are to endure the crucible of the third unit (11.1–16.8) or any shame-ridden 'passions' in their future (13.9-13).

With respect to the 'bread' section of Mark's New Exodus typology (6.31–8.21), an earlier generation of scholars was plagued by the striking similarities in the two feeding episodes (6.31-45; 8.1-9). Some read the two as doublets in a pre-Markan cycle (Achtemeier 1970: 281-84). More recent scholars, especially those influenced by a literary critical orientation argue, however, that the two episodes reveal strategic interests: developing the characterization of the disciples as foils; setting up a contrast between dining ethics at Herod's banquet and the dining ethics of the compassionate shepherd (6.34; 14.27); and anticipating the Passover meal in Mark 14.

Mark certainly has multiple dining scenes, for table-talk and a wider nexus of food imagery permeate the Gospel. From John's diet of locusts and wild honey (1.6) to food and dining related controversies (2.15-27) and from the wilderness feedings of great crowds (6.31-44; 8.1-10) to the Gospel's closing episodes being linked together by a Passover theme, Mark repeatedly signals a 'bread-food-eating theme' (Wegener 1995: 139). In Mark's two wilderness feeding accounts, however, the disciples show that they are not eager to take up a prophetic role. While Jesus is moved repeatedly by compassion, the disciples have to be cajoled to participate in restorative acts. They show here then that they have not fully committed themselves to Jesus' prophetic brand of brokerage, a brand that totally trusts the deity as a sufficient and satisfying source for life's sustenance.

The two feedings in Mark 6 and 8 also stand in contrast to Herod's banquet; this is clearly demonstrated by the similar diction found in all three scenes (see Diagram 7). The juxtaposition of the first two and the inclusion of a third all set up a contrast between two types of brokerage power: the brokerage power of Herod, one of Rome's representatives; and the brokerage power of Jesus, one of the deity's representatives. While both Herod ('the king') and Jesus (a 'shepherd') have the authority, as brokers or those commissioning brokers, to send persons to act (6.17, 27, 30) and to order or command persons to act (6.27, 39), the use of brokerage power by Herod and Jesus could not be more different. In Herod's banquet, power was abused and a rash oath led to a dinner-time execution. In both of the two wilderness feedings, Jesus' actions are motivated on the basis of compassion (6.34; 8.2).

Diagram 7
Similar Diction found in 6.14-29; 6.31-44; and 8.1-9

Herod's banquet	Jesus feeds five thousand	Jesus feeds four thousand
he ordered (6.27)	he ordered (6.39)	_____
'give' cognates (6.22, 23,25,28 [twice])	'give' cognates (6.37 [twice], 41)	'give' cognate (8.6)
John's disciples 'took up' John's body (6.29)	the disciples 'took up' fragments (6.43)	the disciples took up an abundance of fragments (8.8)
'put' or 'place' cognates (6.29)	'put' or 'place' cognates (6.41)	'put' or 'place' cognates (8.6, 7)

As ancient dining practices presupposed boundary markers, only influential persons were invited to Herod's banquet: the great ones, the military commanders (chiliarchs), and the first ones or the leaders in terms of social standing (6.21). By contrast, with the wilderness feedings, Jesus and his followers practiced open commensality to persons who were simply a part of a crowd, a mass gathering of people (6.34; 8.2). Such persons included the uninvited, persons described by Jesus himself 'as those like sheep needing a shepherd' (6.34), and many who had traveled from afar (8.3).

Thus, if Mark's auditors heard the two wilderness feedings as analeptic (as a literary device that makes audiences return to an earlier moment in the narrative), Mark stages a contrast in forms of brokerage. In one form of brokerage, only the powerful are present, and a dinner-time desire puts a prophet's head on a serving platter. In the other, a pious Jesus and his disciples extended hospitality to unknown associates, literally to strangers. On the other hand, if Mark's auditors heard the two wilderness feedings as proleptic (as a literary device that makes audiences anticipate a later moment in the narrative), they would soon learn of yet another time when Jesus would perform a fourfold series of steps (taking, blessing, breaking, and giving) to hark back to the liberative tradition of Passover in ancient Israel's history (14.22). In the last instance, as a 'shepherd' broker (14.27), Jesus would 'give' his body (14.22) and his blood (14.23). Also, just as Herod's 'gift' (*didōmi*) of John's head to the dancing daughter (6.28) eventuated in the 'placing' (*tithēmi*) of John's body (*ptōma*) in a tomb (6.29), even Pilate's 'giving over' (*paradidōmi*) of Jesus to be crucified (15.15) and his 'gift' (cf. *dōreomai*) of Jesus' body (*ptōma*) to Joseph (15.45) eventuated in the 'placing' (*tithēmi*) of Jesus in a tomb (15.46). The two feedings then help Mark to contrast Jesus' Septuagint-based style of brokerage with that of Rome's representatives.

With respect to the 'blindness' section of Mark's New Exodus typology (8.22–10.52), the entire 'blindness' section is framed by two accounts of the healing of a blind man (8.22-26; 10.46-52). Between these two healing accounts, Mark both revisits the question of the identity of Jesus (8.27-30) and includes three passion/resurrection patterns (8.31–10.45). While Mark's 'way' diction throughout the blindness section highlights the New Exodus journey motif, Mark's emphasis on liberation features not only the healings themselves but also Jesus' attempts in the passion/resurrection prediction units to correct the brokerage values of his disciples. So, the healings themselves, as they echo previous parts of the Markan narrative, remind the auditors that Jesus' brokerage power restores bodies counted as broken in the reckonings of ancient societies. The passion/resurrection units critique existing brokerage systems as exemplified either by Herod Antipas (6.14-29) or by Pilate (15.1-15).

In the case of Herod Antipas, one of Rome's representatives, the 'king' uses his brokering power not only to dine with his 'courtiers' (or 'great ones', *megistan*), chiliarchs, and 'the leaders [*prōtoi*] of Galilee' (6.21) but also to grant the dancing daughter's malevolent request. Herod Antipas says to the dancing daughter: 'request (*aiteō*) of me whatever you want (*thelō*) and I will give (*didōmi*) it to you' (6.22). Later, replicating almost the exact diction of Est. 7.2, he says: 'whatever you ask (*aiteō*) me I will give (*didōmi*) you up to half of my kingdom (*heōs hēmisous tēs basileias mou*, 6.24). The daughter, in turn, asks her mother: 'What shall I request (*aiteō*)?' (6.24). Likewise, the narrator remarks that the daughter returned to the king and requested (*aiteō*, 6.25) John's head on a platter. Such a display of brokerage results in John's death even though Herod knows (*oida*) John to be a righteous man (6.20). Herod has made his will that of the daughter and the latter that of Herodias. The result then is a righteous man's death.

In the case of Pilate, another one of Rome's representatives, auditors would see a similar turn of events. Pilate uses his brokerage power, his ability to 'do' something or 'act' (*epoiei*, 15.8; *poieō*, 15.12) on a 'request' (*aiteō*, 15.8), to please the crowd (15.15). That is, he releases the insurgent Barabbas but puts Jesus to death. His brokerage power thus satisfies the crowd's 'wish' (*thelō*, 15.9, perhaps also 15.12), even though the wish was motivated by the chief priests (15.11). Although Pilate 'knows' (*ginōskō*) that the Council was motivated by envy (15.10) when they delivered Jesus, Pilate still grants the crowd's wish, with the result that another good man is put to death.

In the blindness section, Jesus is the broker who has the ability to do what the blind beggar (*prosaitēs*, literally 'one who makes a request', 10.46) wants him to do (10.51). Two of Jesus' disciples also 'want' (*thelō*, 10.35,

36) Jesus as a broker to grant them their request. To the question, 'What do you (plural) want me to do for you?' (*ti thelete [me] poiēsō hymin*), James and John respond with a request for seats of honor (10.35-36). Their 'request' (*aiteō*, 10.35) that Jesus 'grant' (*didōmi*, 10.37) them prestigious seats reveals that their concern for rank and fame, already treated in the second passion/resurrection prediction unit, has not abated. The disciples still want to be 'great' (*meizōn*, cf. 9.34). Thus, Jesus replies that James and John did not 'know' (*oida*, 10.38) what they were 'requesting' (*aiteō*, 10.38) and that what they requested was not his 'to give' (*didōmi*, 10.40). Further-more, he explains that his brokerage style entails the 'giving' of his own life (*didōmi*, 10.45; cf. 8.35).

Thus, the echo-effect from Mark 6 to Mark 10 and eventually to Mark 15 exposes the tyrannical quest of Herod Antipas, Pilate, and even of Jesus' own disciples. Within Jesus' own liberating style of brokerage, Jesus seeks not only to reenact the deity's *liberation of bodies* but also to *liberate the minds* of his disciples, to correct them in preparation for the crucible. Thus, he states: 'You know that among the Gentiles those whom they recognize as their rulers lord it over (*katakurieuō*) them, and their great ones are tyrants (*katexousiazō*) over them. But it is not so among you; but whoever wishes to become great among you must be your servant [or attendant], and who-ever wishes to be first among you must be slave of all' (10.42-44; cf. Col-lins, 1990: 248-52).

So, for the disciples, prophetic brokerage must not be tantamount to advancing in a *cursus honorum*, the standard sequence of magistrative offices that Gentiles pursued for the sake of honor for themselves and their families (Beacham 1999: 34; Edwards 1996: 12-13). Ironically, if Mark's later references to positions on the left and on the right (15.27) are linked to the request by James and John for special seats on the left and on the right (10.37, 40), their request to be seated (or literally to be established with preeminent power) could only be realized as a pure mockery of their quest for elevation, that is, through elevation on a cross. So, for Jesus, to lord over others or to become like a tyrant is to absolutize one's authority and thus to misunderstand one's position as a prophetic mediating figure. Mark's earlier stylization of tyranny in Herod (6.14-29) was then not solely a critique of a brutal so-called 'king'. Rather, it was also a critique of a dis-tinctive brokering style, a type of brokerage that could lead to tyrannical postures among the disciples themselves.

Mark expresses the *lasting* (eternal) nature of Jesus' brokerage style through typological allusions to the Danielic figure known as the Son of the Human One. In the Septuagint text of Daniel, the brokerage term is used plentifully. A voice speaks to Nebuchadnezzar, for example, saying that the God of heaven 'has authority' (*exousian echei*) in the kingdom of people (Dan. 4.31). The Daniel text also notes that at Belshazzar's feast, some persons praised the idols of their hands and did not praise the God of eternity who 'has the authority' (*echonta tēn exousian*) over their spirit (Dan. 5.4). Disturbed by some handwriting on the wall, Belshazzar promises Daniel that he would 'have authority (*echō exousian*) over a third part of my [Belshazzar's] kingdom' if he could interpret the writing (Dan. 5.16). After giving the interpretation, Belshazzar then clothed Daniel in purple and he 'gave authority' (*didōmi exousian*) to him over a third part of his kingdom (Dan. 5.29). Perhaps the most interesting use of *exousia* in Daniel is found in Dan. 7.14. Daniel's auditors are told that 'authority' (*exousia*) was given to the Son of the Human One, an everlasting 'authority' (*exousia*) which would not be taken away (Dan. 7.14). Daniel's auditors also hear about Antiochus IV (the 'ten horns' of the fourth beast or kingdom) into whose 'hands' (*cheir*) the 'holy ones' will be handed over (*didōmi*) for a while (Dan. 7.25). Daniel's auditors also learn that the authority of Antiochus IV ultimately is 'destroyed' (*apollymi*), that is, his 'authority' (*exousia*) is put out of business (Dan. 7.26). Furthermore, Daniel's auditors learn that 'authority' (*exousia*) is 'given' (*didōmi*) to the holy ones (Dan. 7.27). Evidently, then, those with authority in their hands can lose that authority. It can be destroyed and the authority can be given to others.

Daniel's brokerage terminology helps thus to clarify the Son of the Human One expressions in Mark and Mark's use of Daniel to clarify Jesus' brokerage style. Several scholars (Blount 1995: 106; Matera 1982: 105; Vena 2014: 124) group Mark's use of the expression into three different categories: those related to Jesus' 'earthly activity' (2.10, 28); those related to 'suffering', which is the function that predominates (8.31; 9.9, 12, 31; 10.33-34, 45; 14.21, 41); and those related to 'the future coming [arrival]' (8.38; 13.26; 14.62). If we follow the sequential development of Mark's narrative in association with Greek Daniel's references to the Son of the Human One (Greek Daniel 7.13), perhaps there is another way to read Mark's use of the Danielic Son of the Human One. Initially, Mark evokes the Danielic figure when Jesus, the deity's authorized broker (1.22), is embroiled in *verbal clashes* with his stylized opponents (2.10, 28). At this point, then, the expression simply reinforces Jesus' authorized status as a powerful broker, a point the Gospel can make in other ways as Jesus' powerful reenactments of the deity's liberative acts in the past attest.

When the Gospel anticipates contemptuous *physical assaults* on Jesus, Mark repeatedly returns to the Son of the Human One expression (8.31, 38; 9.9, 12, 31; 10.33-34, 45) to justify the possibility that even an authorized figure such as Jesus could face contempt. In fact, Greek Daniel asserts that the 'holy ones' (who are otherwise linked with the Son of the Human One) would be handed over into the hands of Antiochus IV briefly (Dan. 7.25). Mark indicates that the Son of the Human One will be 'handed over' (*paradidōmi*) into the 'hands of men' (*cheires anthrōpōn*, 9.32; cf. 14.41).

At the least, Mark here then appears to have an apologetic goal. The goal is to explain the necessity of the suffering of Jesus as a powerful broker authorized by the deity. Yet another goal may be to nudge the audience to view the contemptuous acts against Jesus in the light of the full temporal scope of the Danielic typology, one that features both the contemptuous handing over of the holy ones *and* their post-contempt exaltation. So, although Jesus will face rituals of humiliation (9.12) on the order of 'holy ones', he must be viewed—in the time of Mark's earliest auditors—from the vantage point of his vindicated status as a resurrected figure associated with power (8.31, 38; 9.9, 31; 10.33-34).

As the narrative comes to a close, Mark links both the coming 'passions' of Jesus' followers (13.9-13) and the 'passion' of Jesus (14.1–15.37) with the Danielic figure who evokes power. Despite the necessity of Jesus being 'delivered up' (*paradidōmi*) in accordance with scripture (14.21), he is to be seen from the vantage point of one who will arrive with 'power' (*dynamis*) and glory (13.26) and as one who is seated at the right hand of 'power' (*dynamis*, 14.62). This is a lasting power. This is a power that will not end.

Summary

Mark depicts Jesus as a teacher but not as one who was a teacher in word alone. Rather, the Gospel portrays this teacher as a powerful broker, as a teacher in word and deed. Viewing Jesus as a powerful broker could well have been yet another way in which Mark's Gospel rehabilitated the image of a crucified Jesus. If crucifixions were designed to show the powerlessness of the victim, to show that the victim did not have the power to save himself (cf. 15.30), the presentation of Jesus as a powerful broker could help to overturn such humiliation.

In making Jesus a powerful broker, Mark had more at stake. Mark's Gospel is not solely *constructive* in the sense of overcoming a tarnished image through the deployment of typologies from the past. Mark's Gospel is also *critical* in its use of such typologies. In the case of its use of brokerage terminology, Mark critiques the brokerage style of Rome's representatives such as Herod Antipas and Pilate. While the brokerage style of these figures is tyrannical (a *lording-it-over* brokerage authority), Jesus' Septuagint-based brokerage style is both *liberating* and *lasting*. Mark's use of Second Isaiah's New Exodus way typology depicts Jesus as an authorized broker who reenacts the deity's liberative acts even as Jesus calls, commissions, and seeks to correct his followers. Mark's use of the Danielic Son of the Human One typology, moreover, depicts Jesus as one who has been given an authority that will not end. The authority that he exercises on earth will continue even beyond his death. Like the holy ones in Daniel, Jesus and indeed a litany of prophets from John to Jesus' disciples will be handed over (1.14; 3.19; 8.31; 9.31; 10.33 [twice]; 13.9, 11-12; 14.10, 18, 21, 41-42, 44; 15.1, 10, 15) to tyrannical figures on the order of Antiochus IV. In the end, though, tyranny will be destroyed. Thus, Jesus' form of brokerage is powerful even if it allows for the realities of the world in which figures like Antiochus wreak havoc on the people of God. Neither in Maccabean times (when Daniel was written) nor Markan times, however, will the Antiochus types prevail. Rather, the authority given by the Ancient One on the Throne to the Son of the Human One is eternal. Thus, again, Mark's narrative is not just a story *about* Jesus or one *for* Jesus' future followers. In its critique of the brokerage system of Rome's representatives, the narrative is also a story *against* the use of abusive power.

Chapter 5

JESUS AS A PHILOSOPHICAL HERO

Introduction

The early Christians who rehabilitated the image of Jesus and that of the larger movement of which he was a part did not desire solely to *defend* Jesus or his movement for the benefit of its adherents. Like other aggrieved groups colonized by Rome, they wanted to *resist* Roman imperial culture with a narrative that featured the exemplary stature of their leaders in the face of a colonizer's dominating forces. A basic strategy for doing so was to deploy a trial type scene where a philosopher faced state power and exhibited heroic signs in the face of death. This well-known strategy of pitting the philosopher against tyrant-like forces was not only apparent in the so-called Greek and Roman periods, but was also deployed by Jews and Christians in and beyond the Second Temple period.

Some writers who deployed the encounter between the philosopher and tyrant also drew on Socrates as a type of rhetorical capital. Could the stylized portrait of Jesus in Mark have been influenced by tales told about the memorable philosopher Socrates? Tales of the latter certainly grew fast and furious, especially those about his final days and conversations as captured by his pupils: Plato, for example, in such dialogues as *Apology* (about Socrates' defense), *Euthyphro* (about Socrates as he awaits his sentence), *Crito* (about Socrates two days before his execution), or *Phaedo* (about Socrates' final hours); and Xenophon, for example, in *Memorabilia* (a depiction of Socrates' own defense) or *Apology* (Xenophon's defense of Socrates; cf. Hägg 2012: 19-27). Through and beyond his earliest pupils, other hagiographical memories of Socrates lived on, including memories of his life before he reached his iconic trial in Athens (Moss 2012: 32-33). In time, the images of successive generations of popular heroes were elevated when they were characterized as having lived, suffered, or died as Socrates did.

This chapter reads the Markan Jesus—the stylized portrait of Jesus in the Gospel of Mark—as a Socratic philosophical hero. While earlier studies have shown that the Gospel of Luke depicts Jesus as a type of Socrates (Sterling 2001: 395-400; Spencer 2008: 50), especially in Luke's 'passion' account', this Guide treads new ground in reading the Markan Jesus as a type of Socratic hero as well. Mark's characterization of Jesus as a philosophical hero facing the tyrant Pilate allowed Jesus to question 'the efficacy and legitimacy of the tyrant's power', which was one of the aims of the philosopher in encountering and challenging a tyrant (Alexander 2002: 249). Also, as foils, Jesus' disciples—not drawn as learning well from their teacher—stumble toward apostasy and appear unheroic—that is, like cowards. If the Gospel of Mark is *about* Jesus and yet *for* Jesus' followers listening to the Gospel, then, they, too, are called to face power in a way that will critique the legitimacy of tyrannical expressions of power. So, again, this is also a Gospel *against* unbridled uses of power.

The Earliest Non-Jewish Instances of the Philosopher vs. Tyrant Typology

The commonplace of the confrontation between a philosopher and a tyrant defiantly questioned who really had power or who truly was a conduit of power. Was true power in the hands of the tyrant who could wield threats or save a potential 'martyr' from the brinks of a sure death? Or, was true power in the hands of the 'wise person' who with endurance refused to cave into the whims and capricious forces of tyranny?

It must be stated initially that anyone could be drawn as a tyrant. That is, although certain Roman emperors (Gaius Caligula, Nero and Domitian) in the Principate were proverbially cast as tyrants, the appellation could be attributed (deservingly or not) to any leader or person with authority and power—kings, proconsuls, military generals (e.g. Lysimachus), governors (e.g. Verres) and so forth (Flinterman 1995: 167; MacMullen 1966: 64; Rawson 1997: 247-49). Ultimately, as indicated in ancient rhetorical handbooks, tragedies, novels, and political invective, the charge could be used rhetorically against any person with power to indicate an abusive use of that power (*Rhetorica ad Herennium*, 2.30.49; Cicero, *De inventione*, 1.53.102; Cicero, *Philippics*, 13.18; Chariton, *Chaereas and Callirhoe*, 1.11.7; cf. Schwartz 2003: 123; Andrews 1997: 469). A tyrant thus was known for libidinal and avaricious excesses (Herodotus, *Histories* 3.31; 3.80.4-5; Euripides, *Suppliants*, 447-55; Plato, *Republic*, 360b-c; Seneca, *Thyestes*, 1046-1047; Suetonius, *Caligula*, 32.1); arbitrary, whimsical, and restraintless uses of power (Herodotus, *Histories* 3.80.4-5; Plato, *Republic*, 572e; Philostratus, *Apollonius of Tyana*, 7.14.4); and the subjection of victims to arrest (Diogenes Laertius, *Lives of Eminent Philosophers*, 9.26, 59), torture (Philostratus, *Apollonius of Tyana*, 7.2.1, 2; Diogenes Laertius, *Lives of Eminent Philosophers*, 9.59), and mockery (Philostratus, *Apollonius of Tyana*, 7.34).

In many instances, including some of the aforementioned ones, the stock image of a tyrant was a part of the antithetical type scene in which a tyrant and a philosopher (or sage) confronted each other (Musurillo 1954: 239; MacMullen 1966: 64). In fact, so widespread was the type scene that it was developed in multiple genres: from funeral laudations, declamatory debate exercises (i.e. mock courtroom speeches), and the *exempla* (lists of exemplary figures from the past) to ancient legends and *Lives* (*bioi*) and the political invective of the Greco-Roman world (Moles 1978: 98; Stoneman 1995: 114; Wills 1990: 71-73).

One of the first extant depictions of this staged scene occurs in Herodotus's account of a sixth-century BCE meeting between the Lydian tyrant Croesus and the sage Solon (Herodotus, 1.29-33; cf. Kennell 1997: 351) in the Greek archaic period. Variations on the type included Herodotus's account of the later meeting between Cyrus and Croesus (now cast as a wise man; Herodotus, 1.86-92), Xenophon's depiction of Hiero of Syracuse and the poet Simonides (*Hiero*, 1.1-11.15; cf. Gray 1986: 119-20; Stoneman 1995: 114), Plutarch's recounting of the meeting between Alexander and Diogenes, along with Lysimachus and Theodorus. The defiance of two philosophers, fifth-century BCE Zeno (against the tyrant Nearchus) and fourth-century BCE Anaxarchus (against the tyrant Nicocreon), were so well-known that multiple authors viewed the two sages 'as models of the way in which philosophers should respond to tyrants' (Sterling 2001: 385-86; cf. Philostratus, *Apollonius of Tyana*, 7.1.2).

In the Roman political period, the confrontation was demonstrated in the encounters between the Roman emperor Nero and Seneca, Nero and other Stoic 'martyrs', the Roman emperors Nero/Domitian and Apollonius in Philostratus's Second Sophistic work *Apollonius of Tyana* (cf. Plutarch, *Alexander*, 14.2; Diogenes Laertius, *Lives of Eminent Philosophers* 6.38 [Wills 1990: 72-73; Flinterman 1995: 167]), and the Roman emperor Hadrian and Secondus the Silent Philosopher.

The Philosopher vs. Tyrant Typology among Aggrieved Jews

Among the Jews, the typology finds palpable expression most famously in traditions that developed about nine Jewish proto-martyrs who resisted Syrian Hellenization, namely, traditions about Eleazar, an unnamed woman, and her seven sons. The earliest record about these proto-martyrs is recorded in what is known as 2 Maccabees. The whole of 2 Maccabees, largely an account of the Maccabean brothers' struggles against Antiochus IV, was either a first-century BCE or first-century CE document written as a part of an epitome of a larger five-volume work by Jason of Cyrene. According to Daniel Joslyn-Siemiarkhosi, this first account 'was a narrative for nationalist Jews that commemorated these [proto-]martyrs as a means of resisting imperial Hellenistic pressures' (2009: 9). Despite the pressures of Antiochus IV who wanted to annihilate the cultural, political, and religious life of the Judeans (2 Macc. 6.1-3), the nine proto-martyrs endure (2 Macc. 6.18–7.42, esp. 6.20). That is, they were willing to suffer (2 Macc. 6.30; 7.18, 32) rather than to concede to the demands of a 'tyrant' (*tyrannos*, 2 Macc. 7.27). They resisted the Seleucid king by refusing to eat pork (which was deemed polluted meat in the Torah), by refusing to concede to the king's enticements (such as a spared life or friendship with the king), and by pronouncing a different metanarrative about power. Declaring Antiochus IV only to have 'authority (*exousia*) among mortals' (2 Macc. 7.16) though he himself was a mortal (2 Macc. 7.16; cf. 9.12), the proto-martyrs by contrast saw their God as Almighty (2 Macc. 6.26; 7.39), one with mighty power (2 Macc. 7.17; cf. 9.8) and the almighty ability to see everything (2 Macc. 7.35; cf. 9.5).

The next record about these nine proto-martyrs was written by an unknown author in what is known as *4 Maccabees*. *4 Maccabees* was a first- or second-century CE philosophical treatise in which the aforementioned proto-martyrs are drawn as philosophers (*4 Macc.* 7.7, 21). They defend or make philosophy credible (*4 Macc.* 5.35; 7.9), or they endure suffering because of it (*4 Macc.* 8.1,15). As in 2 Maccabees, Antiochus IV is depicted as a tyrant (*4 Macc.* 5.4, 14; 6.23; 8.4, 13, 15, 29; 9.1, 3, 15, 30, 32; 10.16; 11.12-13, 21, 27; 12.2, 11; 17.14, 17, 21, 23; 18.5, 20, 22). As in 2 Maccabees, the nine proto-martyrs are known for their 'endurance' (*hypomonē*, 1.11; 5.23; 6.9; 7.9, 22; 9.6, 8, 22; 13.12; 15.30, 32; 16.1, 17, 19, 21; 17.4, 7, 10, 12, 17, 23). Portrayed with recognizable Hellenistic philosophical ideals, the proto-martyrs are cast in a courtroom scene through which they talk back to power and provide examples of the power of reason over emotions. Given its later date of composition, the narrative's critique is not solely against the past actions of the state terror of the Seleucids but also against any unbridled use of power, including that of Rome. As David DeSilva has argued, '[t]he author and addressees share the experience of Roman imperialism in the midst of a region long exposed to Greek imperialism' (2007: 101). As in 2 Maccabees, moreover, the issue of power or might remains critical. Might now is repeatedly viewed as reason's 'rule' (from cognates of the Greek word *kratos*) over pain or the emotions or anything that could cause the proto-martyrs to yield to the tyrant's way of life (1.5-6; 2.6, 9-10, 15, 24; 6.34-35; 7.8; 14.1).

Altogether, these traditions about the Jewish proto-martyrs represent a moment in history when a type of 'minority cultural literature' was used to 'transform experiences of hardship and marginalization' (DeSilva 2007: 344). Such works (along with the *Testament of Joseph*, a mid-third-century to mid-second-century BCE work that lauds patience as a virtue, and the *Testament of Job*, a late first-century CE work that also lauds patience as a virtue) participated in efforts to reconceive how *manliness* could be achieved. Thus, while a passive act such as the endurance of violence would have conservatively been viewed as unmanly, these writings give voice to a long developing ideology of endurance as a noble and manly (courageous) act (Jones 2007: 111-12; Shaw 1996: 276-84). Manliness is no longer reserved strictly for the sphere of the battlefield. It has shifted both to athletics (cf. Dio Chrysostom, 29.8) and to the internal, moral sphere of passively enduring any kind of dangerous situation with equanimity (Jones 2007: 123). A key figure helping to shape that shift was Socrates, to whom this chapter now turns.

The Socratic Philosophical Hero

When writers in or near the New Testament period depicted philosophers who suffered or died while resisting tyrants, some of their depictions were influenced by a Socratic model, at least as idealized by Plato (Sterling 2001: 387) and by Xenophon of Athens. Indeed, Xenophon's portrait of the encounters between Hiero of Syracuse and the poet Simonides (*Hiero*, 1.1–11.15) may have been the first of many Socratizations of the meeting of a tyrant and a philosopher. Later, Seneca's depiction of a valiant Cato the Younger reading Plato's *Phaedo* and taking his own life rather than capitulating to the strongman Julius Caesar evoked Socrates' desire to remain true to his principles at death as he was in life (Seneca, *Epistles*, 24.6-8). Also, according to Tacitus, many of the acts of Seneca himself in the wake of Nero's order that Seneca commit suicide evoked similar actions taken by Socrates in his final days. Seneca consoled friends; he took the hemlock; and, similar to Socrates offering a cock to the healing god Asclepius, he offered a libation to Jupiter (Tacitus, *Annals*, 15.63.4-64.5). Furthermore, Epictetus's portrait of the Roman Senator Helvidius Priscus's bold and testy exchange with Vespasian (who had threatened him with exile and death) also evoked Socrates' fearlessness (Epictetus, *Discourses* 1.2.19-21).

Thus, the sufferings or deaths of popular figures were often elevated to a heroic status when they were characterized as having suffered or died as Socrates did. Socrates, then, was a type of rhetorical capital. Already widely valued as a hero, Socrates, or better, images of the final days of Socrates could be overlaid on the images that particular communities had already bequeathed to their famous leaders. The overlay on the one hand could add to the stature of the famous local leader because that leader now appeared to have suffered or died nobly. On the other hand, the overlay could strengthen one of the goals of the philosopher vs. tyrant encounters, namely, the exposure of the lack of real power in the tyrant. In the aforementioned encounters, the tyrant was not victorious. The tyrant could not control the image of courage left behind by the 'philosopher' type.

Yet, how did Socrates become a hero? In its earliest Greek iterations, the term hero (derived from the Greek word *hērōs* in the singular form or *hērōes* in the plural) referred to a martial figure seeking eternal renown through a noble death on the battlefields of war, as with Homer's Achilles in the *Iliad* (9.406-420). For the sake of such 'renown' (*kleos*, *Iliad* 9.415), Achilles chooses to 'remain' (*menō*) in the battle against the Trojans and to accept the ultimate 'end-goal' of life (his *telos*, *Iliad* 9.411, 416), though doing so would mean that he would never return home (*Iliad* 412). Homer's Odysseus in the *Odyssey* was also a hero. While he did not die in battle and did return home to Ithaca, he was as much a hero because of the pains he endured (*menō*, *Odyssey* 5.362) or the 'toils' (*ponoi*, *Odyssey* 13.301; 20.49; 23.249), 'labors' (*aethloi*, *Odyssey* 1.18; 4.170; 4.241; 23.248, 350), and wanderings (*Odyssey* 10.150; 11.160-67; 13.90-91; 15.175-77; 16.204-206) that he suffered (*Odyssey* 8.155), including a descent to the underworld, which mimicked the act of dying. As such, Odysseus endured the type of ordeals (*Odyssey* 11.617-22) that Heracles 'endured' (*hypomenō*, Diodorus Siculus 1.2.4; 4.1.4-6). Heracles faced 'labors' (*aethloi*, *Iliad* 2.8.363), including his descent to the underworld (*Iliad* 9.76-138). He was also the Greek 'hero *par excellence*' (Finkelberg 1995: 5). The first Greek heroes thus were mortal beings 'male or female, of the remote past, endowed with superhuman abilities and descended from the immortal gods themselves' (Nagy 2013: 9). In epic literature, all such heroes were known for their 'martial efforts' (*aethlos*; cf. Nagy 2013: 270). Some, like Heracles, also became immortal.

While Achilles as a hero won the 'glory of being remembered forever' (Nagy 2013: 12) through his death on the battlefield and while Odysseus was heroic through his toils, labors, and wanderings, athletes could also be heroes. One of Heracles' labors was his victorious competition in every athletic event at the first Olympics in 776 BCE (Nagy 2013: 40; cf. Diodorus Siculus 4.14.1-2; Croy 1998: 43). Also, various myths about athletic competitions in the prestigious Panhellenic games (from the Olympic games to the Pythian games and the Nemean games) were established to 're-enact a prototypical ordeal...of a hero' (Nagy 2013: 269). Thus, as Gregory Nagy explains: 'In the inherited diction of praise poetry...the *aethlos* (*athlos*) [or "ordeal"] ...is applicable both to the athletic event of the athlete in the present and to the life-and-death struggle of the hero in the past' (2013: 12). Furthermore, the word *agōn*, which is derived from the verb *agō* ('I lead' or 'I gather') literally means 'a "bringing together" of people' and is the basis for our words 'antagonist' and 'agony' (Nagy 2013: 271). To compete then is to re-enact a heroic struggle from the past (Nagy 2013: 271). Victorious athletes (derived from the Greek word *athlētēs*) then competed to win public recognition for themselves and for their hometowns in the fifth century BCE athletic contests as celebrated in the poet Pindar's encomia to the winners of Panhellenic games.

Although Socrates' end did not come on battlefields or in great games, multiple dramatizations of the Athenian sage gave Socrates heroic characteristics. How then did he become a hero? First, a key characteristic of the heroic stature of Socrates was his belief that a divine imperative was on his life, which was 'a standard heroic trope' (Hook and Reno 2000: 52), Thus, in the Socratic tradition, through the use of cognates of the impersonal verb *dei* ('it is necessary'), Socrates repeatedly speaks of the necessity of his death (*Crito* 43b, 43d, 44a). In the *Apology* Socrates also sees himself as a gift of the deity (*Apology* 30d) and as one who was attached to the city of Athens by the deity (*Apology* 30e). Also, whether or not the whole of the *Apology* is a Socratic 'mission statement' (Hunter 2012: 116), the militaristic language of stations or posts in the *Apology* exposes Socrates' view of his philosophical mission in the face of death: 'For wherever someone stations (*tassō*) himself, thinking it to be best or he was stationed (*tassō*) by a commander, there he must (*dei*) remain (*menō*) to face danger, taking into consideration neither death nor anything except shame [of retreat]' (*Apology* 28d; cf. Weiss 2006: 249). After acknowledging the stations of his military service for Athens and how he 'remained' (*menō*) at the post assigned by his Athenian military commander, Socrates deduces that it would be impossible out of a fear of death to 'leave' (*leipō*) the 'station' (*taxis*) given to him by God or the philosophizing life to which he was 'bound' (*dei*) by God (*Apology* 28e). Elsewhere, when the interlocutor Laches avers that the courageous person is someone 'who is willing to stay at his post (*taxis*) and face the enemy and does not run away (*pheugō*)', Socrates also concedes that a person is 'courageous' (*andreios*) if he 'stays' (*menō*) at his 'post' (*taxis*) and fights the enemy (*Laches* 191A), though he moves the sphere of courage beyond the limited venue of the battlefield (cf. 191D) and he qualifies courage by insisting that it be attached to wisdom (192B).

A second feature contributing to Socrates' heroic status was his prescience about the future, including his own death (Plato, *Apology* 30c-d; 63c5-6; *Crito* 43b, 54e; cf. Xenophon, *Memorabilia* 4.8.9-10). Socrates was composed throughout his ordeal because he knew what would happen in the future. In the *Apology* he anticipates that an attempt to 'injure' (*blaptō*) him would actually injure Athens (30c). Also, he is aware that his 'hour (*hōra*) has come' (Plato's *Apology* 42a), which, according to Gregory Nagy, was a critical marker of the hero. As Nagy notes, 'the very idea of the ancient Greek hero is defined by *hōra* as the right 'time' of death. Death then is not a surprise but an expectation' (2013: 614). Thus, Socrates, according to Xenophon, was able to deliberate 'concerning his defense and the end (*teleutēs*) of his life' (Xenophon, *Apology* 1.3; cf. 5.3; 9.5; 23.2; 26.4; cf. Plato, *Phaedo* 117e, 118a). Furthermore, in what may have been a 'post-eventum' farewell prophecy, Socrates anticipates that after his death many would follow him to examine the Athenians more intensely (*Apology* 39b-d;

cf. Hunter 2012: 115). Thus, his farewell prophecy includes his own death and its consequences for Athens. Perhaps, it is also a charter or foundation account for those who will follow him. That is, it gives them a legitimate role in the Athenian world (Hunter 2012: 115).

A third feature contributing to Socrates' status as a hero was his refusal to escape from prison or save himself from death. The aforementioned military imagery that depicts the divine imperative on Socrates' philosophizing mission also emphasizes his endurance or his refusal to leave his post. Instead, he vows to remain at his post without regard to any kind of danger or the possibility of death. Even were his release or acquittal possible on the terms that he would not philosophize, Socrates candidly would deny the terms of the acquittal. 'I will obey the deity rather than you, and as long as I would have breath (*empneō*)... I will in no way cease philosophizing' (*Apology* 29d; my translation). In several instances in *Crito*, Socrates rejects Crito's plea for Socrates 'to save' (*sōzō*) himself from an inevitable death by escaping (*Crito* 44b-c; 45a-b; 46a).

Finally, a fourth feature contributing to Socrates' heroic status was his courage or fearlessness in the face of death (Plato, *Apology* 28b, 38d-e; *Phaedo* 68c-d, 117c). In fact, even in the face of death, he had the ability to console family and friends (*Phaedo* 60a, 116a-b). Others 'marveled' (*thaumazō*) at his 'cheerfulness and calmness' (Xenophon, *Memorabilia* 4.8.20).

Thus, while Socrates faced a series of humiliating rituals—from arrest to imprisonment to false charges and a 'judicial execution'—his innocence and his courage became a model for subsequent generations far and wide (Reeve 1989: 108). His way of suffering and dying, then, became a new heroic model—a philosophical model—for the subsequent proto-martyrs and martyrs.

Variations on the Socratic Hero in the Roman World

Writers in the Roman period were not straightjacketed by a Socratic impulse (Whitmarsh 2001: 141-51). Musonius Rufus, a type of Roman Socrates, for example, adopted and adapted a Socratic persona. Although he was a Roman citizen, Musonius Rufus (or someone using his persona) wrote in Attic Greek (the Greek of elites in the Greek East), imbibed Greek culture, and rewrote the Greek past as a participant in a broader cultural effort to resist Rome's political dominance. Thus, he invoked yet adjusted such classical traditions as *parrhēsia* or 'freedom of speech' (as expressed in Euripides), the quest for knowledge through travel (as represented by the Homeric Odysseus), the inversion of social roles (as expressed in traditions about Diogenes, the Cynic), and a willingness to face injustice with integrity (as expressed by Socrates). While Socrates of old refused to leave

Athens (the city that opposed him), Musonius Rufus as the Roman Socrates resisted Nero's injustice by exercising free speech and practicing philosophy in exile away from Rome (the city that opposed him).

Given that Socrates died by drinking hemlock (which could have been understood as a painless exit), Stoic philosopher Seneca admires Socrates but adds more 'pain' in his accounting of Socrates' death (Wilson 2007: 129). In discussing the political suicide of Seneca (among others), the Roman historian Tacitus also focuses on 'pain', especially the protracted blood-letting that Seneca endured as he otherwise followed Socrates' model of drinking hemlock and offering a prayer to a god (Wilson 2007: 130-34).

Anecdotes that developed about the nine Jewish proto-martyrs who resisted Syrian Hellenization also adjusted the Socratic tradition. Assuredly, the final days of the Jewish proto-martyrs were in sync with the Athenian pedagogue's view of a divine imperative on his life. Thus, after describing Eleazar as one who was in harmony with the law and as the philosopher of divine life, *4 Maccabees* (which expands 2 Macc. 6.12–7.42) avers that such action is necessary (*dei*) for those who do the work of the law (*4 Macc.* 7.7).

Furthermore, in *4 Maccabees*, the narrator deploys military diction to describe the character of the proto-martyrs just as that diction was deployed in the Socratic traditions. The narrator describes Eleazar like a city able to withstand the attacks of diverse siege engines because of reason (*4 Macc.* 7.4). The eldest brother encourages all of his brothers not to 'leave their posts or station' (*leipotakteō*) but to 'fight' (*strateuō*) as soldiers engaged in a 'fight' (*strateia*) for religion (*4 Macc.* 9.23-24).

Prescience was also a feature of the Jewish proto-martyrs. In 2 Maccabees, the seven brothers and their mother repeatedly speak of resurrection as their vindication (2 Macc. 7.9, 11, 14, 23, 29, 36). Tongues and hands lost to torture will be reclaimed (2 Macc. 7.11). Life and breath lost to torture will return again (2 Macc. 7.21-23). Likewise, the proto-martyrs acknowledge that Antiochus will be tortured (2 Macc. 7.17) and will not be able to escape the hands of God (2 Macc. 7.31, 35-36). Similarly, in *4 Maccabees*, the proto-martyrs were able to endure unspeakable horrors because they were certain about the future, a future that would vindicate them but destroy the tyrant (9.8, 32; 10.10, 21; 11.3; 12.12, 14; 13.17). Like Socrates, the band of brothers also knew that the tyrant could not really 'injure' (*blaptō*) them (*4 Macc.* 9.7).

Similarly, although the proto-martyrs face horrific pain, as shown in *4 Maccabees*, they never recant even when the offer to save themselves is made repeatedly to Eleazar (*sōzō*, *4 Macc.* 5.6; 6.15; cf. 6.27) and to the seven (*sōzō*, *4 Macc.* 10.1; *sōze seauton*, *4 Macc.* 10.13; *sōtērion*, *4 Macc.* 12.6; cf. *4 Macc.* 15.26-27; Philostratus, *Apollonius of Tyana* 7.36.1). They refuse any offers to be 'released', that is, acquitted (*apoluō*, 2 Macc. 6.22,

30; *4 Macc.* 8.2; 11.13). Moreover, they viewed any deliverance offered by their captors as but temporary 'safety' (*sōtērion*, *4 Macc.* 15.8, 27).

Also, as with Socrates, the courage of the proto-martyrs also evokes 'amazement' (*thaumaston*). Though old in age, for example, Eleazar evoked amazement (*4 Macc.* 7.13). The mother of the seven also was admired for her courage (2 Macc. 7.20; *4 Macc.* 14.11). According to *4 Maccabees*, all people, including the torturers of the nine proto-martyrs, marveled at their courage and endurance (*4 Macc.* 1.11; cf. 17.17), as if the proto-martyrs were athletes in a competition. That is, the proto-martyrs describe their suffering as if it were a race or a contest for which they would receive an 'athletic prize' (*athlon*, *4 Macc.* 9.8; cf. 17.12) for their endurance (*hypomonē*). Eleazar is called a noble 'athlete' (*athlētēs*) who, though, being 'beaten' (*tuptō*) was conquering his tormentors (*4 Macc.* 6.10). The brothers perceive their experiences of torture as a 'contest' (*agōn*), as if they had been summoned to the 'bodily training' (*gymnasia*) of 'hard labors' (*ponos*, *4 Macc.* 11.20). They are described as 'competitors of virtue' (*aretēs agōnistas*, *4 Macc.* 12.14) and as 'running a course' (*hodon trechontes*, *4 Macc.* 14.5). Their mother herself is described as one who obtained the athletic prize of the contest (*agōn*, *4 Macc.* 15.29). Encouraging her sons, she remarks: 'My sons, noble is the *contest* (*enagōnisasthe*) to which you are called to *bear witness* (*diamarturia*) for the nation' (*4 Macc.* 16.16). Thus, all nine are to be 'admired' (*thaumazō*) as 'athletes of divine legislation' (*4 Macc.* 17.16) who—in their contention for the athletic 'crown' (*stephanousa*, *4 Macc.* 17.15)—literally faced Antiochus as their 'antagonist' (*antagōnizō*, *4 Macc.* 17.14) with the world and humanity as the spectators or 'observers' (*theōreō*, *4 Macc.* 17.14).

A key difference between many of the Socratic traditions and the depictions of the nine proto-martyrs, however, is that the anecdotes about the proto-Jewish martyrs are narrated with *detailed* accounts of the torture that the proto-martyrs received. Socrates never faced torture.

Many interpreters have noted Luke's distinctive characterization of a Socratic Jesus in the closing scenes of that Gospel's lore (for example, Sterling 2001: 395-400; Spencer 2008: 50). Luke presents Jesus, for example, as a calm, innocent, and paradigmatic figure in the face of death. When arrested, he is resolute (Lk. 22.53). When Jesus is tried, Luke repeatedly acknowledges Jesus' innocence (Lk. 23.13-15, 22, 41, 47). At death's door, the Lukan Jesus does not cry out 'My God, my God, why have you forsaken me' in Greek or Aramaic, as he did in Mark (Mk 15.34; cf. Ps 21.1 LXX). Rather, he declares in dauntless tones: 'Father, into your hands I entrust my spirit' (Lk. 23.46).

Both Socrates and the Lukan Jesus appear to have met their fates in similar circumstances. For Socrates, as best we can tell, prominent and powerful citizens of Athens brought him to trial and falsely accused him of impiety

and the corruption of youth (Plato, *Euthyphro*, 2c; 3b; *Apology* 19b3-c1;
30c-d; cf. Xenophon, *Memorabilia* 1.1.1–1.2.64; Diogenes Laertius, *Lives
of Eminent Philosophers* 2.40.3-7). Luke gives a similar picture, with Jesus
accused by the Sanhedrin and brought before Pilate (Lk. 22.54–23.2). In
his farewell speech in Plato's *Apology* moreover, Socrates acknowledges
the injustice of his accusers: he speaks of their 'wickedness and *injustice*'
(*adikia*), *Apology* 39B4-5), compares himself to others who also faced an
'unjust trial' (*krisis adikos*, *Apology* 41B2), and reckons that false accusation and envy ultimately were the catalysts behind his death (*Apology* 28a;
cf. 18d; Xenophon, *Memorabilia* 3.9.8). Again, Luke exposes the injustice
of those who, though in charge of meting out justice, made a mockery of
it. Knowing the innocence of Jesus, Pilate still hands Jesus over to be crucified. Pilate does so, moreover, in a context in which he releases a known
criminal (Lk. 23.25).

Like other writers, the Lukan author did not use the Socratic traditions in
a wholesale fashion. Rather, the author presented Jesus as a philosophical
hero whose humiliation and pain are put on display to describe the established authorities as being out of control. Jesus faces mockery and insults
by his captors (Lk. 22.63-65). Also, although Pilate recognizes the Lukan
Jesus' innocence, Herod's soldiers treat Jesus with contempt (Lk. 23.11)
and Pilate still considers flogging Jesus (Lk. 23.16). Furthermore, while
Luke's Gospel is not as graphic with its presentation of Jesus' crucifixion,
the event is still a spectacle of shame: he is crucified with criminals (Lk.
23.33), mocked by soldiers (Lk. 23.36), and derided by one of the criminals (Lk. 23.39).

The Markan Jesus and the Typology of the Socratic Hero

Did the Lukan author who otherwise appears to follow Mark simply decide
to take a fresh approach in presenting a Socratic Jesus? Or, is it possible that
Luke's fuller use of Socratic ideals in the Gospel of Luke and in the Book
of Acts (e.g. the Lukan author's presentation of the early witnesses, Stephen, and Paul [Alexander 1993: 31-64]) actually was influenced by Mark?
Would a close and careful reading of Mark's Gospel reveal a characterization craft that also was influenced by Socratic ideals?

While Mark also was not straightjacketed by the typology of the Socratic
hero, some parts of Mark do bear a striking resemblance to Socratic traditions. First, the Markan Jesus also appears to have had a divine imperative on
his life and death, as the impersonal verb *dei* would substantiate (8.31). In the
litany of occurrences associated with the verb *dei*, Mark speaks of the necessity of Jesus' suffering, rejection by established figures, and death. By comparison, the disciples, as led by Peter, claim that they would die with Jesus
if it were necessary (*dei*, 14.31), but three of them do not 'remain' (*menō*)

watchful in prayer (14.34) and the actions of all of the disciples fall short (14.50).

Second, the Markan Jesus is also endowed with prescience to understand his hour and the hour for others that will follow him. Like Socrates, Jesus is aware of his hour (*hōra*) or approaching death (14.35, 41). Throughout Mark's Gospel, the narrative exposes Jesus' true power by granting him the ability to predict the suffering that he would ultimately face. His ability to anticipate his death (2.20) and to indicate vividly in passion/resurrection prediction units (8.31–9.1; 9.30-50; 10.32-45) how a series of 'deliveries' (14.10-11, 18, 21, 41, 44; 15.2, 10, 15) would lead to a 'mocking and flogging' conclusion reveals not only the 'shadow of death' (Donahue 1995) that rested like a canopy over the entire narrative, but also how someone else—neither Antipas nor Pilate, Rome's brokers—was actually in control. He also knows the lot expected for his followers who are told to endure to the end (*telos*, 13.13)

Third, the Markan Jesus does not seek escape in the crucible scenes of his life. Well aware that he will be rejected, he goes with others from Galilee to Jerusalem, the place of rejection. His public acts on the entrance way to Jerusalem and subsequently in the temple (where he is disruptive) certify that he will not seek escape. Though he initially asks that the cup be removed from him, he ultimately accepts the will of the deity (14.36). Nor does he adhere to the 'save yourself' mockeries of the passersby on the day of his judicial execution: within the whole of the mockery charade in Mark 15, onlookers request that Jesus save himself (15.30-31), a request on a par with Pilate's request for Jesus to answer charges brought against him, though Jesus refuses to answer (15.3-5).

Finally, although Mark certainly did not evoke Socrates as wholeheartedly as did Luke to depict Jesus' final days, Mark still seems to evoke Socrates' calm in the face of death. Mark does so, though, not with the initial grief of Jesus in Gethsemane but with the resolute way with which Jesus' Gethsemane prayer ends. As Yarbro Collins has noted, 'the prayer concludes with the serene acceptance of God's will; the finishing touches on the portrait thus call to mind Socrates and those who follow his example in meeting death with composure and courage' (2007: 635). Furthermore, while some scholars are reluctant to separate the centurion's declaration of Jesus as the Son of God (15.39) from the repeated instances of mockery that precede it, auditors familiar with heroic traditions would be able to interpret the centurion's declaration as another example of the astonishment of those who look on the noble suffering and death of a hero. Thus, the centurion could well be drawn as someone 'that acknowledges Jesus' extraordinary status as a hero or a ruler' (Yarbro Collins 2007: 770).

Thus, Mark seems to appeal to a variety of Socratic features to depict Jesus as a Socratic hero, as one who died well. If so, Mark reshapes Jesus' ignominious death by figuring that death as a valiant one. Jesus' good exit, however, does not occur without the raw description of a man experiencing intense pain. Jesus' last words ('My God, my God, why have you forsaken me?' in 15.34), a shrieking edition of Psalm 22, testify to Jesus' venting anguish through the use of scripture (Yarbro Collins 2007: 753). One must note, moreover, that Jesus' anguish is mentioned in the context of a description of portents. Such portents—whether the descending darkness or the rending of the temple's veil—are indicators of a good man's death. That is, such portents are linked 'with the accounts of the deaths of famous people' (Yarbro Collins 2007: 752). Mark's earliest auditors would likely have taken Jesus' way of dying as yet another example of his heroic modeling in that he refused a pain palliative (as would be a typical act of resistance for noble deaths, 15.23; cf. Yarbro Collins 2007: 743). Finally, the plea 'My God' at the end of his ministry virtually frames the Gospel with the words 'my son' spoken by a voice from heaven when Jesus began his ministry (1.11). Thus, Jesus dies as he lived, in an intimate relationship with God.

Summary

Mark, like other writings that drew on the philosopher vs. tyrant typology, wrote back to power by illustrating the courage of heroic figures even as Mark exposed injustice and the lack of control of Rome's brokers. When Mark gives extended treatment to the suffering and death of John and Jesus in Mark 6 and 14-15 respectively, the Gospel does so to describe the character of these two prophetic emissary brokers as models for auditors who— like John and Jesus—will be brought before councils, kings, and governors (Mark 13). In the case of Jesus, the scene of confrontation also featured Socratic images that overlay the tale of Jesus. Still, Mark does not strictly rely on the heroic mold of the larger Greek and Roman cultures of the time. Rather, Mark also portrays John and Jesus as mistreated prophets. In the case of Jesus, Mark will allow the auditors to see how the heroic Jesus faced and conquered an 'internal struggle' with death in Gethsemane (Tolbert 1990: 267-72) before Jesus stood resolutely before his captors. Thus, Jesus is not portrayed, in Senecan terms, as having a 'lust for death' (Seneca, *Epistles* 24.25), but he is resolute after an initial struggle.

Who has power? Mark writes back to turn the gaze upon the oppressors. Mark does not shy away from the brutality, the sheer horror, and the humiliation of a decapitated head on a dinner platter or the gory and gruesome scenes of a staged 'king' tried, whipped, mocked, and crucified. In such presentations, Mark points out the raw, whimsical, and unjust nature of power when directed at persons who otherwise are deemed righteous and innocent. Using the type scene of the tyrant and the philosopher, Mark mocks Rome and presents John and Jesus as examples for auditors who are told that salvation will come to 'the one who has endurance' (*hypomenō*, 13.13). The Gospel of Mark, like *2 Maccabees* and *4 Maccabees*, the *Testament of Joseph*, and the *Testament of Job* are all a part of a shift in the ideological reckoning of endurance as a worthy way of facing danger and responding to powerful figures. For *2 Maccabees* and *4 Maccabees* and for the Gospel of Mark, moreover, that danger may come because of tyrants or their henchmen.

CONCLUSION

The basic argument of this Guide is that the Gospel of Mark deploys general rhetorical strategies (such as a rhetoric of descent, a rhetoric of deeds, and a rhetoric of dying well), and multiple specific typologies (or stereotyped character constructions such as a prophetic envoy type, a powerful broker type, and a philosophical hero type) in its characterization of Jesus. Furthermore, the Guide has argued that Mark deploys such general rhetorical strategies and specific typologies for three reasons. In part, the author of the Gospel aims to write *about* Jesus to help its earliest auditors know that Jesus and his movement were not failures despite some criticism that may have followed in the wake of Jesus' ignominious type of death. The Gospel, as with most works that became a part of the New Testament writings, struggled then to rehabilitate the image of Jesus from a shameful death. In part, the author of the Gospel of Mark also aims to write *for* Jesus' followers, for those who likely experienced their own shame-ridden difficulties in the kinds of circumstances that Jesus predicted for his followers in his farewell apocalyptic discourse, especially in Mk 13.9-13. The basic problem facing the Markan auditors then was not an errant Christology but that of marginalization, alienation, arrest, detention, and trial if Mk 13.9-13 is a transparent witness to the profile of such auditors. In part, the author of the Gospel of Mark further aims to write *against* the abuse of power that Jesus' followers faced at the hands of Rome's representatives. Mark's 'passion' of John (Mk 6.17-29) and the 'passion' of Jesus (Mark 14–16) spoke volumes against the tyranny of Rome's representatives who used their brokerage power not to aid others but to lord over those already aggrieved.

The earliest Markan auditors would have heard Mark's narrative as a story of rejection—the rejection of John, of Jesus, and ultimately of Jesus' disciples (within and potentially outside of the narrative). In the flow of the narrative, John is the first prophetic messenger to be rejected. Whisked off the narrative stage early on in the Gospel (1.14), John meets his fate when an on-going grudge of Herodias, the dinner-time tyrannical tactics of Herod Antipas, and the desire of the dancing daughter all lead to John's beheading (6.14-29). Jesus himself acknowledges that 'they [i.e. select forces of opposition] did to him [John, a type of Elijah figure] whatever they wanted' (9.13). The Markan narrator patently adds later that the Jerusalem authorities did not accept John's baptism as a baptism authorized by God (11.31).

As soon as John is 'handed over' or 'delivered up' (*paradidōmi*, 1.14) to the authorities, Mark presents a protracted account of yet another authorized messenger who eventually is 'handed over' or 'betrayed' (3.19; 9.31; 10.33 [twice]; 14.10-11, 18, 21, 41-42, 44; 15.1,10, 15). In more intimate spaces (8.31; cf. 9.31; 10.30ff), Jesus directly and openly speaks about his 'rejection' as the Son of the Human One (or, more familiarly, the Son of Man, cf. Blount 1995: 106; Vena 2014: 124). Nor does he change his tune in crucible scenes where tough opponents follow and repeatedly pester him in more public spaces (12.10). Throughout the Gospel, Jesus faces rejection of one sort or another: by those who question his authority near the beginning (2.7, 10) or ending of the Gospel (11.28, 33), by scribes that come down from Jerusalem to attribute Jesus' power to a preeminent diabolical force (3.22), by Gerasenes who fail to offer the basic rudiments of hospitality to the stranger in their midst (5.1-19), by on-and-quickly-off-again-wailers who deride Jesus with laughter (5.38-40), and even by a home-town crowd in a synagogue at Nazareth, where Jesus laments the fate of all prophets ('A prophet is not without honor except in his own country and among his own kin and in his own house', 6.1-6a, esp. 6.4, NRSV).

According to Jesus' predictions, his disciples can also expect to be a part of the 'delivered up' series that befalls prophetic messengers (13.9, 11-12). Even if some of Jesus' disciples possibly faced earlier rejection on journeys to proclaim repentance and to cast out demons (Mk 6.6b-13), they can still expect to be brought before kings and governors (13.9ff). Indeed, the very act of following Jesus entails rejection—the general exigencies of 'persecutions' (10.30; cf. 4.17) and separation from Jesus, the shepherd (14.27), but also the possibility of facing a cross (or the ultimate experience of shame, 8.34).

As this Guide has shown, at the heart of Mark's Gospel lies the goal of preparing auditors to take on prophetic stances in their own times of tyrannical pressure, in those times when they are 'delivered up'. Mark builds resisting auditors through an extended tale about two paradigmatic prophets, John and Jesus, who remained faithful to the very end. In the case of Jesus, for which the writer likely had more information, Mark provides compelling details about the authorization of Jesus as a prophetic envoy, a powerful broker, and a philosophical hero who took on a valiant stance in the crucible throes of provincial authorities and Rome's representative, Pilate, in Jerusalem. Mark's extended tale weds basic tyrant vs. philosopher encounters to additional anecdotes that reveal the sum and substance of prophetic character, namely, resistance to any but the deity of Israel's scriptural tradition. Furthermore, inasmuch as Mark seeks to build disciples, a story that mostly narrates Jesus' professional life is told from the perspective of disciples. That is, Mark's acoustical arrangement depicts Jesus calling, commissioning, and correcting disciples in preparation for a prophetic stance in the crucible, the most intense moments of the Gospel narrative.

So, if the auditors are 'built' by the narrative, if the story persuasively prepares them to be prophetic, the Gospel's art of resistance will have achieved its goal. The Gospel does not endorse taking up arms. It does not endorse siding with the political rebels (or armed freedom fighters) who might have been frequently resisting Rome in the late 60s and early 70s of the first century CE. Instead, this story—which Mark calls the beginning of the good news—seems to presuppose that the simple witness and proclamation of the good news to all the nations in the currents of 'trials' or 'passions' (13.9-10) is the right course for those awaiting the coming of the Son of the Human One.

If this Guide has made a good case for the aforementioned claims, contemporary interpreters must ask some tough questions both about Mark's approach to characterization and about the ethics of Mark's characterization for life today. Mark's approach to characterization is not an historical approach that provides verifiable information on what Jesus really said or what Jesus really did. Instead, Mark's approach is typological, based on stereotyped character constructions that the author of Mark and Mark's earliest auditors would have known. The typologies noted in this study— and the author of Mark likely used yet others—are visible because scholarship has been able already to see the importance of such types in a world in which everyone was constantly negotiating power claims. The author of Mark thus depicts Jesus with familiar, strategically nuanced typologies that would convince the Gospel's earliest audiences of the continuing impact of Jesus's life despite his tragic death, their difficult circumstances, and the Roman-backed forces of tyranny that Jesus and his movement had experienced. Whoever Jesus *was* for Markan auditors then was what Jesus *needed to be* to help a struggling minoritized group survive in the Roman world of power. The Gospel was never history. It was only a response to the tough circumstances of the people who first heard it.

Beyond Mark's approach to characterization, there is also the problem of the ethics of the Gospel for today's readers. Since the Gospel's production and first performances, depictions of Jesus' social identity have continued to be what various communities needed Jesus to be. If anything has changed, it is that the power dynamics of Jesus' once prophetic movement have changed and continue to evolve. Contemporary hearers and readers of Mark's Gospel must be careful then in assuming that the Gospel can *easily* be applied to today's circumstances if such hearers and readers do not have the minoritized constraints on their lives as the earliest Markan auditors once had.

From an ethical perspective, contemporary audiences must also think carefully about the Gospel's ideology of suffering. While the Gospel's story, especially when appreciated as a creative and complete one, is a moving narrative about courage under pressure, its narrative poses some problems for those who seek to embrace its ideology of suffering fully today. Thus, while I have long admired the Gospel, I wish to conclude this Guide by asking auditors and readers to think about three ethical implications of this Gospel and its rhetoric about suffering.

First, the Gospel's approach to suffering is shot through with dichotomous diction about losing to save, being last to be first, and being slave of all vs. being the greatest. In the course of the narrative, the goal of such paradoxical diction is to change the mindset of the disciples, those who would prepare themselves for crucible moments. Fair enough! Yet, this countercultural diction seems best directed only to folks who have never been last or those who have never been enslaved (cf. Tolbert 1995). Unfortunately, this kind of diction has often led many to seek out perpetual lowly stances as a way of being like Jesus. The likely prophetic edge of the diction, though, is not to create more people at the low end of social hierarchies but to challenge nepotistic and tyrannical values that only served Rome and the elite.

Second, if the Gospel's emphasis on endurance or passive acceptance of suffering (as depicted by Jesus on the cross) is a correct understanding of the Gospel's message, that message hardly aids those who have been perennially taught that their suffering is the will of God (which is a possible reading of Mark's view of Jesus' death in 14.36) or that their passive suffering will end when the Son of the Human One returns.

Third, Mark's view of endurance as a type of manliness and its view of cowardice as unmanliness (at least in accord with the logic of the day) is built on misogynistic codes that should not be tolerated in our own times.

Let me hasten to say, though, that I still relish much that is good in Mark—its resistance to tyranny, its parade of resilient, active characters (the so-called 'little people') who refuse to be quieted, shunned, or shut out, and its message about the need to develop a whole community of prophetic voices to challenge existing systems of degradation and exploitation. For those in our own times who can look at the Gospel with both a critical eye and a heart of conviction, this once misunderstood story may still speak good news across the ages. Let the reader—any reader—understand!

Works Cited

Achtemeier, Paul J.
   1970   'Toward the Isolation of Pre-Markan Miracle Catenae', *JBL* 89: 265-91.
Aernie, Jeffrey W.
   2012   *Is Paul Also among the Prophets? An Examination of the Relationship be-tween Paul and the Old Testament Prophetic Tradition in 2 Corinthians* (London: T. & T. Clark).
Alexander, Loveday
   1993   'Acts and Ancient Intellectual Biography', in *The Book of Acts in Its Ancient Literary Setting* (ed. Bruce W. Winter and Andrew D. Clarke; Grand Rapids, MI: Eerdmans): 31-64.
   2002   '"Foolishness to the Greeks": Jews and Christians in the Public Life of the Empire', in *Philosophy and Power in the Graeco-Roman World. Essays in Honour of Miriam Griffin* (ed. Gillian Clark and Tessa Rajak; Oxford: Oxford University Press): 229-49.
Andrews, S.B.
   1997   'Enslaving, Devouring, Exploiting, Self-Exalting, and Striking: 2 Cor. 11.19-20 and the Tyranny of Paul's Opponents', in *SBL 1997 Seminar Papers* (Atlanta. Society of Biblical Literature): 460-90.
Ascough, Richard S.
   2008   'Forms of Commensality in Greco-Roman Associations', *Classical World* 102: 33-45.
Aune, David
   1987   *The New Testament in its Literary Environment* (Philadelphia: Westminster Press).
Barasch, Moshe
   2001   *Blindness: The History of a Mental Image in Western Thought* (New York: Routledge).
Beacham, Richard C.
   1999   *Spectacle Entertainments of Early Imperial Rome* (New Haven, CT: Yale University Press).
Bederman, David K.
   2001   *International Law in Antiquity* (Cambridge: Cambridge University Press).
Bernstein, Neil W.
   2003   'Ancestors, Status, and Self-Presentation in Statius' *Thebaid*', *Transactions of the American Philological Association* 133: 353-79.
   2008   *In the Image of the Ancestors: Narratives of Kinship in Flavian Epic* (Toronto: University of Toronto Press).
Black, C. Clifton
   2001   *Mark: Images of an Apostolic Interpreter* (Minneapolis, MN: Fortress Press).

Blount, Brian K.
  1995   *Cultural Interpretation: Reorienting New Testament Criticism* (Minneapolis, MN: Fortress Press).
Bowersock, G.W.
  1994   *Fiction as History: Nero to Julian* (Berkeley: University of California Press).
Bradley, A.C.
  1949   *Shakespearean Tragedy: Lectures on Hamlet, Othello, King Lear, Macbeth* (London: Macmillan, 2nd edn).
Bryan, Christopher
  1993   *A Preface to Mark: Notes on the Gospel in its Literary and Cultural Settings* (New York: Oxford University Press).
Burnett, Joel S.
  2010   '"Going down" to Bethel: Elijah and Elisha in the Theological Geography of the Deuteronomistic History', *JBL* 129: 281-97.
Burridge, Richard
  2004   *What Are the Gospels? A Comparison with Graeco-Roman Biography* (Grand Rapids, MI: Eerdmans, 2nd rev. edn).
Coleman, Kathleen
  1990   'Fatal Charades: Roman Executions Staged as Mythological Enactments', *JRS* 80: 44-73.
Collins, John J.
  1990   'The Sage in the Apocalyptic and Pseudepigraphic Literature', in *The Sage in Israel and the Ancient Near East* (ed. John G. Gammie and Leo G. Perdue; Winona Lake: Eisenbrauns): 343-54.
  2007   *A Short Introduction to the Hebrew Bible* (Minneapolis, MN: Fortress Press).
Collins, John N.
  1990   *Diakonia: Re-interpreting the Ancient Sources* (New York: Oxford University Press).
Compton, Todd
  1990   'The Trial of the Satirist: Poetic Vitae (Aesop, Archilochus, Homer) as Background for Plato's Apology', *AJP* 111: 330-47.
  2006   *Victim of the Muses: Poet as Scapegoat, Warrior, and Hero in Greco-Roman and Indo-European Myth and History* (Washington, DC: Center for Hellenic Studies).
Croy, N. Clayton
  1998   *Endurance in Suffering: Hebrews 12.1-13 in its Rhetorical, Religious, and Philosophical Context* (SNTSMS, 98; Cambridge: Cambridge University Press).
Davis, Dale Ralph
  1984   'The Kingdom of God in Transition: Interpreting 2 Kings 2', *Westminster Theological Journal* 46: 384-95.
DeSilva, David
  2007   'Using the Master's Tools to Shore up Another's House: A Postcolonial Analysis of 4 Maccabees', *JBL* 126: 99-127.
De Temmerman, Koen
  2007   'Where Philosophy and Rhetoric Meet: Character Typification in the Greek Novel', in *Philosophical Presences in the Ancient Novel* (ed. J.R. Morgan and Meriel Jones; Groningen: Barkhuis Publishing): 85-110.

Dillon, Richard J.
    1995   '"As One Having Authority" (Mark 1.22): The Controversial Distinction of
            Jesus' Teaching', *CBQ* 57: 92-113.
Donahue, John R.
    1973   *'Are You the Christ?': The Trial Narrative in the Gospel of Mark* (Missoula,
            MT: Society of Biblical Literature).
    1982   'A Neglected Factor in the Theology of Mark', *JBL* 101: 563-94.
    1995   'Windows and Mirrors: The Setting of Mark's Gospel', *CBQ* 57: 1-26.
Donahue, John R., and Daniel J. Harrington
    2002   *The Gospel of Mark* (Collegeville, MN: Liturgical Press).
Dowd, Sharyn
    2000   *Reading Mark: A Literary and Theological Commentary on the Second Gos-
            pel* (Macon, GA: Smyth & Helwys).
Edwards, Douglas
    1996   *Religion and Power: Pagans, Jews, and Christians in the Greek East* (New
            York: Oxford University Press).
Farmer, William R.
    1964   *The Synoptic Problem: A Critical Analysis* (New York: MacMillan).
Finkelberg, Margalit
    1995   'Odysseus and the Genus "Hero"', *Greece and Rome* 2: 1-14.
Flinterman, Jaap-Jan
    1995   *Power, Paideia and Pythagoreanism* (Amsterdam: J.C. Gieben).
Forster, E.M.
    1927   *Aspects of the Novel* (New York: Harcourt, Brace and Co.).
France, R.T.
    2002   *Gospel of Mark: A Commentary* (Grand Rapids, MI: Eerdmans).
Freudenburg, Kirk
    1993   *The Walking Muse: Horace on the Theory of Satire* (Princeton, NJ: Princeton
            University Press).
Fuhrmann, Christopher J.
    2012   *Policing the Roman Empire: Soldiers, Administration, and Public Order*
            (Oxford: Oxford University Press).
Funk, Robert
    1959   'The Wilderness', *JBL* 78: 205-214.
Gray, V.J.
    1986   'Xenophon's *Hiero* and the Meeting of the Wise Man and Tyrant in Greek
            Literature', *Classical Quarterly* 36: 115-23.
Grünewald, Thomas
    2004   *Bandits in the Roman Empire: Myth and Reality* (London: Routledge).
Hägg, Tomas
    2012   *The Art of Biography in Antiquity* (Cambridge: Cambridge University Press).
Harker, Andrew
    2008   *Loyalty and Dissidence in Roman Egypt: The Case of the Acta Alexandrino-
            rum* (Cambridge: Cambridge University Press).
Harvey, W.J.
    1965   *Character and the Novel* (Ithaca, NY: Cornell University Press).
Hoffmeier, James K.
    2005   *Ancient Israel in Sinai: The Evidence for the Authenticity of the Wilderness
            Tradition* (New York: Oxford University Press).

Holzberg, Niklas
 1993 'A Lesser Known "Picaresque" Novel of Greek Origin: The *Aesop Romance* and its Influence', in *Groningen Colloquia on the Novel*, V (ed. H. Hofmann; Groningen: Egbert Forsten): 1-16.

Hook, Brian S., and R.R. Reno
 2000 *Heroism and the Christian Life. Reclaiming Excellence* (Louisville, KY: Westminster/John Knox Press).

Horsley, Richard A.
 2001 *Hearing the Whole Story: The Politics of Plot in Mark's Gospel* (Louisville, KY: Westminster/John Knox Press).
 2003 *Jesus and Empire: The Kingdom of God and the New World Disorder* (Minneapolis: Fortress Press).
 2011 *Jesus and the Powers: Conflict, Covenant, and the Hope of the Poor* (Minneapolis: Fortress Press).

Hunter, Richard
 2012 *Plato and the Traditions of Ancient Literature: The Silent Stream* (Cambridge: Cambridge University Press).

Johnson, Luke Timothy
 1986 *The Writings of the New Testament: An Interpretation* (Philadelphia: Fortress Press).
 1989 'The New Testament Anti-Jewish Slander and the Conventions of Ancient Polemic', *JBL* 108: 419-41.

Jones, Meriel
 2007 'Andreai and Gender in the Greek Novel', in *Philosophical Presences in the Ancient Novel* (ed. J.R. Morgan and Meriel Jones; Groningen: Barkhuis Publishing): 111-35.

Joslyn-Siemiarkhosi, Daniel
 2009 *Christian Memories of the Maccabean Martyrs* (New York: Palgrave Macmillan).

Jouanno, Corinne
 2009 'Novelistic Lives and Historical Biographies: The *Life of Aesop* and the *Alexander Romance* as Fringe Novels', in *Fiction on the Fringe: Novelistic Writing in the Post-Classical Age* (ed. Grammatiki A. Karla; Leiden: Brill): 33-48.

Kähler, Martin
 1964 *The So-Called Historical Jesus and the Historic Biblical Christ* (Philadelphia: Fortress Press).

Keith, Chris
 2011 *Jesus' Literacy: Scribal Culture and the Teacher from Galilee* (New York: T. & T. Clark).

Kelber, Werner
 1976 'From Passion Narrative to Gospel', in *The Passion in Mark: Studies on Mark 14–16* (ed. Werner H. Kelber; Toronto: Macmillan): 153-80.
 1983 *The Oral and the Written Gospel: The Hermeneutics of Speaking and Writing in the Synoptic Tradition, Mark, Paul, and Q* (Philadelphia: Fortress Press).

Kennell, Nigel M.
 1997 'Herodes Atticus and the Rhetoric of Tyranny', *Classical Philology* 92: 346-62.

Knowles, Michael P.
    1993   *Jeremiah in Matthew's Gospel: The Rejected-Prophet Motif in Matthaean Redaction* (Sheffield: JSOT Press).
Lefkowitz, Mary R.
    1981   *The Lives of the Greek Poets* (Baltimore, MD: The Johns Hopkins University Press).
Lendon, J.E.
    1997   *Empire of Honour* (New York: Oxford University Press).
Luke, Trevor
    2010   'Ideology and Humor in Suetonius' *Vespasian*', *Classical World* 103: 511-27.
MacMullen, Ramsay
    1966   *Enemies of the Roman Order: Treason, Unrest, and Alienation in the Empire* (Cambridge: Harvard University Press).
Malherbe, Abraham J.
    1985   '"Not in a Corner": Early Christian Apologetic in Acts 26.26', *Second Century* 5: 193-210.
    1989   *Paul and the Popular Philosophers* (Minneapolis: Augsburg Fortress Press).
Marcus, Joel F.
    1992   'The Jewish War and the *Sitz im Leben* of Mark', *JBL* 111: 441-62.
    2006   'Crucifixion as Parodic Exaltation', *JBL* 125: 73-87.
    2009   *Mark 8–16: New Translation with Introduction and Commentary* (New York: Doubleday).
Mason, Steve, and Micheal W. Helfield
    2008   *Josephus, Judea, and Christian Origins: Methods and Categories* (Grand Rapids, MI: Baker Academic).
Matera, Frank J.
    1982   *The Kingship of Jesus: Composition and Theology in Mark 15* (Chico, CA: Scholars Press).
Matthews, Victor H.
    2012   *The Hebrew Prophets and their Social World. An Introduction* (Grand Rapids, MI: Baker Academic).
McRae, Rachel
    2011   'Eating with Honor: The Corinthian Lord's Supper in Light of Voluntary Association Meal Practices', *JBL* 130: 165-81.
Mitchell, Margaret M.
    1992   'New Testament Envoys in the Context of Greco-Roman Diplomatic and Epistolary Conventions: The Example of Timothy and Titus', *JBL* 111: 641-62.
Moles, J.L.
    1978   'The Career and Conversion of Dio Chrysostom', *Journal of Hellenic Studies* 98: 79-100.
Morgan, J.R.
    1993   'Make-Believe and Make Believe: The Fictionality of the Greek Novels', in *Lies and Fiction in the Ancient World* (ed. Christopher Gill and T.P. Wiseman; Austin: University of Texas Press): 175-229.
Moss, Candida R.
    2012   *Ancient Christian Martyrdom: Diverse Practices, Theologies, and Traditions* (The Anchor Yale Bible Reference Library; New Haven, CT: Yale University Press).

Musurillo, Herbert (ed.)
1954   *The Acts of the Pagan Martyrs: Acta Alexandrinorum* (Oxford: Clarendon Press).
Nagy, Gregory
2013   *The Ancient Greek Hero in 24 Hours* (Cambridge, MA: Belknap).
Nickelsburg, George W.E.
1980   'The Genre and Function of the Markan Passion Narrative', *HTR* 73: 153-84.
Notopoulos, James A.
1951   'Continuity and Interconnexion in Homeric Oral Composition', *TAPA* 82: 100-101.
Pao, David W.
2000   *Acts and the Isaianic New Exodus* (Tübingen: Mohr Siebeck).
Peppard, Michael
2011   *The Son of God in the Roman World: Divine Sonship in its Social and Political Context* (New York: Oxford University Press).
Perkins, Pheme
2007   *Introduction to the Synoptic Gospels* (Grand Rapids, MI: Eerdmans).
Pervo, Richard I.
1994   'Panta Koina: The Feeding Stories in the Light of Economic Data and Social Practice', in *Religious Propaganda and Missionary Competition in the New Testament World: Essays Honoring Dieter Georgi* (ed. Lukas Bormann, Kelly Del Tredici and Angela Standhartinger; Leiden: E.J. Brill): 163-94.
2008   *The Mystery of Acts: Unraveling its Story* (Santa Rosa, CA: Polebridge).
Rawson, Elizabeth
1997   'Roman Rulers and the Philosophic Adviser', in *Philosophia togata. I. Essays on Philosophy and Roman Society* (ed. Miriam Griffin and Jonathan Barnes; New York: Oxford University Press): 233-58.
Reeve, C.D.C.
1989   *Socrates in the Apology: An Essay on Plato's Apology of Socrates* (Indianapolis, IN: Hackett).
Rhoads, David, Joanna Dewey and Donald Michie
1999   *Mark as Story: An Introduction to the Narrative of a Gospel* (Minneapolis, MN; Fortress Press, 2nd edn).
Roller, Matthew B.
2001   *Constructing Autocracy: Aristocrats and Emperors in Julio-Claudian Rome* (Princeton, NJ: Princeton University Press).
Satterthwaite, Philip E.
1998   'The Elisha Narratives and the Coherence of 2 Kings 2–8', *Tyndale Bulletin* 49: 1-28.
Schwartz, Saundra
2003   'The Trial Scene in the Greek Novels and in Acts', in *Contextualizing Acts: Lukan Narrative and Greco-Roman Discourse* (ed. Todd Penner and Caroline Vander Stichele; Atlanta: Society of Biblical Literature): 105-37.
Scott, Gary Allen
2000   *Plato's Socrates as Educator* (Albany, NY: SUNY).
Seo, J. Mira
2013   *Exemplary Traits: Reading Characterization in Roman Poetry* (New York: Oxford University Press).

Shaw, Brent D.
    1996   'Body/Power/Identity: Passions of the Martyrs', *Journal of Early Christian
            Studies* 4: 269-312.
Shiner, Whitney T.
    1998   'Creating Plot in Episodic Narratives: The *Life of Aesop* and the Gospel
            of Mark', in *Ancient Fiction and Early Christian Narrative* (ed. Ronald F.
            Hock, J. Bradley Chance and Judith Perkins; Atlanta, GA: Scholars Press):
            155-76.
Smith, Abraham
    2006   'Tyranny Exposed', *BibInt* 14: 259-93.
Spencer, F. Scott
    2008   *The Gospel of Luke and Acts of the Apostles* (Nashville: Abingdon Press).
Stanton, Graham N.
    1992   *A Gospel for a New People: Studies in Matthew* (Edinburgh: T. & T. Clark).
St Clair, Raquel
    2008   *Call and Consequences: A Womanist Reading of Mark* (Minneapolis: For-
            tress Press).
Sterling, Gregory
    2001   '*Mors philosophi*: The Death of Jesus in Luke', *HTR* 94: 383-402.
Stoneman, Richard
    1995   'Naked Philosophers: The Brahmans in the Alexander Historians and the
            Alexander Romance', *Journal of Hellenic Studies* 115: 99-114.
Struthers Malbon, Elizabeth
    2009   *Mark's Jesus: Characterization as Narrative Christology* (Waco, TX: Baylor
            University Press).
    2012   'Mark', in *The Women's Bible Commentary* (ed. Carol A. Newsom, Sharon
            H. Ringe and Jacqueline E. Lapsley; Louisville, KY: Westminster/John Knox
            Press, revised and updated edn): 478-92.
Talbert, Charles
    1977   *What Is a Gospel? The Genre of the Canonical Gospels* (Philadelphia: For-
            tress Press).
Tannehill, Robert
    1980   'Tension in Synoptic Sayings and Stories', *Interpretation* 34: 138-40.
Tell, Håkan
    2011   *Plato's Counterfeit Sophists* (Washington, DC: Center for Hellenic Studies).
Tolbert, Mary Ann
    1990   'The Gospel in Greco-Roman Culture', in *The Book and the Text: The Bible
            and Literary Theory* (ed. Regina Schwartz; Oxford: Basil Blackwell): 258-
            75.
    1992   'The Gospel of Mark', in *Women's Bible Commentary* (ed. Carol A. Newsom
            and Sharon H. Ringe; Louisville, KY: Westminster/John Knox Press, expanded
            edn): 350-62.
    1995   'When Resistance Becomes Repression', in *Reading from This Place. II.
            Social Location and Biblical Interpretation in Global Perspective* (ed. Fer-
            nando F. Segovia and Mary Ann Tolbert; Minneapolis: Fortress Press): 331-
            46.
    1996   *Sowing the Gospel: Mark's World in Literary-Historical Perspective* (Minne-
            apolis: Fortress Press).

Trocmé, Etienne

1975 *The Formation of the Gospel according to Mark* (trans. Pamela Gaughan; Philadelphia: Westminster Press).

Vena, Osvaldo D.

2014 *Jesus, Discipleship of the Kingdom: Mark's Christology for a Community in Crisis* (Eugene, OR: Wipf & Stock).

Watts, Rikki

2000 *Isaiah's New Exodus in Mark* (Grand Rapids, MI: Baker Books).

Wegener, Mark I.

1995 *Cruciformed: The Literary Impact of Mark's Story of Jesus and his Disciples* (Lanham, MD: University Press of America).

Weiss, Rosalyn

2006 'Socrates: Seeker or Preacher?', in *A Companion to Socrates* (ed. Sara Ahbel-Rappe and Rachana Kamtekar; Malden, MA: Blackwell): 243-72.

Welch, John J.

1981 'Introduction', in *Chiasmus in Antiquity: Structure, Analyses, Exegesis* (ed. John W. Welch; Hildesheim: Gerstenberg): 8-15.

Wheatley, Alan B.

2011 *Patronage in Early Christianity: Its Use and Transformation from Jesus to Paul of Samosata* (Eugene, OR: Pickwick).

Whitmarsh, Tim

2001 *Greek Literature and the Roman Empire: The Politics of Imitation* (Oxford: Oxford University Press).

Wills, Lawrence M.

1990 *The Jew in the Court of the Foreign King: Ancient Jewish Court Legend* (Minneapolis: Fortress Press).

Wilson, Emily

2007 *The Death of Socrates* (Cambridge, MA: Harvard University Press).

Yarbro Collins, Adela

2007 *Mark: A Commentary* (Hermeneia; Minneapolis, MN: Augsburg Fortress Press).

INDEX OF SUBJECTS

INDEX OF AUTHORS